$\frac{3}{3}$

16

$\%=$

THE HEART OF JESUS

BEING ADDRESSES UPON

THE PRESENT REALITY OF THE PASSION

GIVEN IN ST. PAUL'S CATHEDRAL
AT THE MIDDAY SERVICES IN HOLY WEEK, AND AT THE
THREE HOURS' DEVOTION OF GOOD FRIDAY, 1901,

BY

P. N. WAGGETT, M.A.

SOCIETY OF ST. JOHN THE EVANGELIST

TENTH THOUSAND

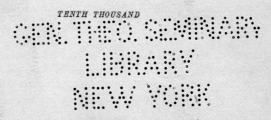
LONDON
SOCIETY FOR PROMOTING
CHRISTIAN KNOWLEDGE
1920

To

MY DEAR AND MOST LOVING

MOTHER,

BY WHOSE SIDE I FIRST TOOK PART

IN THE DEVOTION OF THE THREE HOURS,

AND FROM WHOSE LIPS I LEARNED

THE NAME WHICH IS ABOVE EVERY NAME,

THE HOLY, SAVING, AND EVER-BLESSED NAME OF

JESUS.

PREFACE

I TAKE this occasion to offer my thanks
to the Very Reverend the Dean and the
Reverend Chapter of St. Paul's, by whom I
was permitted to share the Holy Week Devo-
tions of the Cathedral; to the venerable
Society which invited and authorized the
present publication; and to my kind friend,
Mr. G. E. Hall, who, when he was quite unknown to me, made a full shorthand report
of the addresses, and with a ready generosity
which I have since proved in many instances,
placed his careful transcript freely at my
disposal.

I have done what other duties permit me
to do towards making the sentences clear.
The general aspect of the addresses must
remain quite different from that of a written
composition.

If there is anything in these pages which appears doubtful, I do not—at least at this time, or in this form—contend for it. Let whatever appears reasonable and plain be taken for what it may be worth.

In what I have said of the Ransom paid by our Divine Saviour (pp. 10, 28, etc.), I hope I have kept within the words of Holy Scripture. In respect of the allied and combined, but not necessarily identical truths of Redemption, Purchase, and Ransom, we need a study of Scriptures, by review, co-ordination, and especially analysis, even more searching than the many which have been published. The *deliverance of mankind* which our Lord effected by His Death was a work of *Power*, and the dyeing of His garments the sign of victorious conflict. That rescue was typified by the overthrow of Egypt and the passage of the Red Sea. There was no price paid to Satan ; he was spoiled as Pharaoh was spoiled ; and the Holy Life was paid down as the soldier's life is paid down in the work of rescue—life for life, the hero's life for the life of the oppressed. "The Son of

Man came to give His life a ransom for many"
(Matt. xx. 28); "A ransom for all" (1 Tim.
ii. 5).

But in the Passion there was a mystery of
true Purchase, and the Precious Blood was and
is a price. The Purchase was the purchase of
the *Church*, which our Lord bought for Himself, not from God but unto God (Rev. v. 9);
and the treasure was paid to alienated souls
that they might be no longer "their own"
but "bought with a price" (1 Cor. vi. 19, 20),
"not with silver and gold," as a bride was bought
by an earthly husband, "but with the precious
blood of Christ as of a lamb without blemish
and without spot" (1 Pet. i. 18, 19). The
price was paid *for possession*. Christ is our
Master—δεσπότης—Whom we may not disown,
our "Master that bought" us (2 Pet. ii. 1) to
be His slaves (1 Cor. vii. 23). He is the Lord
Who has given Himself for the Church, "that
He might present it to Himself" (Eph. v. 25,
27), "the Church of God which He hath purchased with His own blood" (Acts xx. 28).
He is the Bridegroom—the title is reserved in

the ancient Scriptures to God—Who claims
"the Bride the Lamb's wife" (Rev. xxi. 9),
because He has "purchased unto God with
His blood men of every tribe and tongue and
people and nation" (Rev. v. 9).

The substance of the Introductory Address
of Good Friday is contained in what was said
on Monday and Tuesday.   From my point of
view it was necessary to repeat it in presence
of a congregation practically new to me.

P. N. W.

Ditchingham,
  St. Etheldreda's Day, 1901.

CONTENTS

		PAGE
I.	MONDAY IN HOLY WEEK	11
II.	TUESDAY IN HOLY WEEK	23
III.	WEDNESDAY IN HOLY WEEK	39
IV.	THURSDAY IN HOLY WEEK	58
V.	GOOD FRIDAY	75
	THE FIRST WORD	83
	THE SECOND WORD	93
	THE THIRD WORD	103
	THE FOURTH WORD	114
	THE FIFTH WORD	125
	THE SIXTH WORD	135
	THE SEVENTH WORD	141

I

MONDAY IN HOLY WEEK

"For there is one God, one Mediator also between God and men, Himself man, Christ Jesus, Who gave Himself a ransom for all; the testimony to be borne in its own times; whereunto I was appointed a preacher and an Apostle."—1 Tim. ii. 5-7.

To-day I propose simply to consider something of the purpose of the Holy Week, and the method of keeping it. The text, in spite of certain difficulties which you will suppose have not been left unconsidered, may be taken to refer to two realities—the facts of our Lord's Passion, and the testimony which is borne to those facts in their own season. From time to time, in proper seasons, by Apostles appointed, and in the Church which fulfils as a whole the apostolic function, there is borne the due testimony, and the effective working testimony, to the saving facts of our Lord's redeeming death. There are the two points: first, the Lord's redeeming death. "He gave Himself, being a Mediator between God and man, Himself man—He gave Himself to be

a ransom," ἀντίλυτρον, a ransom equivalent,[1]
and equivalent in nature, equivalent to all
mankind. He gives life for life, His life for
all those lives. And in the second place, this
act of His giving is testified to in a saving
manner; so that people are lifted out of sin
and death into life and righteousness by the
fulfilment, age after age, of the apostolic duty
of bearing testimony to the death of Jesus.
This is the purpose which Holy Week in
part fulfils. Holy Week belongs to that great
work of witness. It is a solemn and organized
and church-wide bearing of that testimony of
the death of Christ which is able, when received, to save men's souls. Therefore it is
good for us to consider how best, or rather in
what fashion among many equally good, we
may make this week a real one to ourselves.

There must be in the first place always the
great work of memory—the work of reading
and hearing and knowing the sacred record of
the Lord's death. And so, behind every other
kind of exercise in Holy Week—more fundamental than all our prayers and offices, lies
the reading of the Scripture which is set down
for us morning after morning in the Holy
Liturgy. That is the base and fundamental
necessity of a good Holy Week—to give ourselves to the hearing, or according to our

[1] See Preface, p. vii.

opportunity to the reading, of the inspired record of the way in which Christ died. And that, although it is so very simple and obvious a duty to be fulfilled according to our opportunities, is nevertheless one which at this moment needs to be emphasized. For we hear everywhere—and it is a wholesome cry—of the superiority of the inward to the outward. It is indeed a stirring hope of our moment, this return to the inward sphere of reality which is in man's consciousness. But because of that penury of our nature which always leads us to think that to gain one good thing we must lose some other good thing—a mood of mind which comes from the natural narrowness of our circumstances in this world— because of this, there is abroad an opinion that we shall more firmly grasp and know and enjoy the inward presence and power of Jesus Christ if we disparage, and turn our backs upon, the historical records of the ancient saving facts. Amiel is quoted afresh : "The great need of the age is a translation of Christianity out of the sphere of history into the sphere of psychology,"—which means that we are to persuade ourselves and each other to look for and to cultivate Christian moods in the heart, and to be indifferent to the reality of the great facts in the world long ago, and in Heaven and earth now. It becomes us Chris-

tians, therefore, to say that we shall find the
security of this inward knowledge and saving
power of Christ nowhere else, unless we find it
also in an "historical" belief that He really
took our flesh upon Him; and, being Himself
Man, actually in the sphere of common facts, in
history, worked out the salvation which to-day
the believer is to find and cherish and live
upon in his secret heart. The first part, then,
of the work of Holy Week is the memory, the
acceptance, the renewal of our knowledge, of
these sacred, saving facts as they are recorded
for us in the Gospels.

Then in the second place—and this also is,
of course, very familiar to all Christians—there
is the great work of the affections. And it is
precisely in contrast to this work of the affections that I would state the method which I
beg you especially to consider. Not that we
should in any way, or need in any way, disparage that work of sensitive feelings and warm
imagination and almost dramatic representation of the death of Christ. All that, in the
inspired body of the Church, and done according to the will of the Holy Spirit energizing
in the Church, is a real and blessed help
towards bringing the soul and mind into con-
tact with the Redeemer Who loves us. But
every one who has spent many Holy Weeks—
who has gone on year after year in something

like faithful devotion during this week, and year after year has knelt on Good Friday, and striven to raise up his mind and heart by imagination in sympathy with the Saviour— knows something of the danger and the difficulty about which I would speak for one moment; the danger, that is to say, of feeling that our strong and warm sensations and ideas, our love and our sorrow, can only be maintained at their height by resolutely forgetting matters of fact. This method of devotion, good as it is, lies under the threat of so simple and so inevitable a danger as the revealing by our memories of what goes on outside the door. "Christ is before us," you say with your historical present. You speak of Him as going from place to place, as doing the great acts this week. And all the while—even on Good Friday—the common man, rich or poor, the wise men and the simple, the busy people and the thoughtful, are haunted by this answer, "Yes, but it is not so. After all, to-day is as yesterday. As for our God, He is to-day in Heaven just as yesterday, just as after next Sunday He will be." There is the perpetual threatening of the incoming of criticism into this method of devotion which relies upon a warm imagination and a loving spirit of sensitive affection. That danger is a real danger. And it is a sad pity that we should attempt

to get rid of it by crushing down and putting
out of sight the obvious fact that this Monday
in the first week of April is for God, precisely
like last Monday, precisely like the Monday
which we usually call, after the day of Resurrection, Easter Monday. Our God is to-day
in Heaven even as before, and those old facts,
though we speak of them as if they were
repeated before our eyes, are not, indeed,
repeated any more ; for He has once died, and
having died unto sin once, He is in Heaven,
alive for evermore in the substance of His
sacred human nature—alive for evermore to
the glory of God the Father !

We do well, then, to consider a third
method, this third real link between us and our
Divine Saviour, which will stand all the stress
of common sense, of ordinary experience ;
which will not faint when sensitive affection
begins to flag ; which will not sink when the
imagination grows cool, but stands firm in the
reality of present facts.   What are the present
facts which this week, and on Good Friday
especially, we can enter into ? They are briefly
the present fact of the sin and need of man
and the present fact of the Heart of our Lord
Jesus Christ. This last is a fact not outside
our apprehension, as is the fact of God's most
holy Being, which we adore, but cannot come
near to so as to understand it ; in the Lord's

Heart—God and man—in His human affection, is a fact which in one sense is in the same order as our own hearts, as our own experience day by day; which together with its human accessibility has obtained a divine permanence, has been filled—through the power of the Word, through the will of the Father, by the operation of the Holy Ghost—has been filled with the perpetual abiding continuance and fulness of life which belong to the Heavenly order and to the throne of God. So then before us to-day and to-morrow, and all this week, there lies the Heart of Jesus Christ. And, you will say, this week is the same as other weeks. And I reply, the Holy Week is given us in order that by means of the pointers, if I may so speak, which are given to us in the memory of the sacred facts, and by means of those other directors which are in our own wants, our own hearts, we may penetrate all the mist of ages, all the cloud of sins, and come up to where Jesus Christ waits for us, "the same yesterday and to-day and for ever"; and yet in such wise the same that there is in Him somewhat, a reality of fact, which rightly and truly and actually corresponds with, and is the perpetual fountain of, those actions and those sufferings which He accomplished in that week of which Holy Week is the memory. There, in Christ, in the fulness

B

of His heart, are those qualities, those movements of the soul, those realities of spiritual being, which were the fountain-head of His suffering, of His willingness to die for us. For to every single detail of the sorrow and the pain there answers an abiding reality in the Heart of Jesus Christ to-day. And starting from our Church-memory of what He did, by pondering over the record, we arrive at a communication very much higher than that of personal memory—much more real than that of excited feelings or of warmed imagination; we find a road in the Holy Spirit Himself, in the sphere of His operation; we enter a path which will lead us gradually, step by step, back to where Christ, up to where Christ waits for us, pouring out from His Heart the very movements, the real spiritual activities which were the cause of all the separate actions of His Passion and Death. Thus in succeeding days we may really find the true substance of each of those things which in Holy Week are put before us. We come to the true substance of His sacrifice, for it is now flowing out from His Heart. We come to the true substance of His Passion, for the reality of His Passion is still in His Heart. We are come to the true pity for sinners which nailed Him to the Cross, for that is still moving towards us. And so coming, as we look up and pray for the Holy

Ghost, as we seek to see Him with our hearts, and beg that the eyes of our understanding may be opened, we are brought into the very law and rule which governed the Passion itself. For the Passion itself, as we may perhaps find an opportunity to say, is a fact altogether of the heart. In its true reality it rests upon the laws of love. "Thou sayest," one of our new poets has sung, "Thou sayest this law ordains relief all other laws above— That earth cannot contain its grief, nor Heaven contain its love." That was the law which brought Christ down from Heaven; that was the strong impulse which led Him to the Cross; and we, entering into movements and realities of the same kind, shall find Him actually present to our hearts. Along the path of the history, along the path of the recorded actions, we shall find our way back, not to some fanciful representation of His Person, nor to some vision of His standing before us, but we shall come to the secret of His Heart, to the true reality, to the true Jesus Christ, to the real power of God's love which answers to the requirements of our real hearts.

"O healing face," cries the same poet— whom faith can welcome as a new ally, and who did not always, I think, stand quite clearly on our side in the conflict with sense and the world—

"O Healing Face, to all mankind most kind,
  Teach me to find Thee, lest I wander blind!
  For as the river seeks the sea, And as its rest the rain,
  So seeks my face for Thee, So pleads my prayer the
      pain
  That pleads through Thee:
  'Behold and see,
  Is there a sorrow that has no part in me?'" [1]

And to conclude, because it is founded upon His pity and our grief, because this method of coming to God lies in the law, and according to the operation, of His own real motives in loving us, therefore it is secure, and therefore also it is easy for us. It is hard for us to stir again the tinglings of imagination, but it is easy for us to find again, to sink again into our wretchedness, to know again our need or, not knowing it, to groan out the groan that cannot be uttered. There in the heart lies the hollowness which Jesus Christ can fill. We then in this week are called upon for no straining of the intelligence, that we should strive might and main to understand things too hard for us; we are called upon for no magic of imagination that by some cultivated mood, or by some shrouded room, or by some unnatural silence, we should avail to imagine ourselves in the fleshly presence of Jesus Christ. But we have only to leave off our battling with ourselves, to cease to

[1] Laurence Housman, *Spikenard.*

silence that cry which can neither be stilled
nor uttered, to let the heart tell those things it
cannot tell, to let it ache out its ache, and in
its aching it finds already Jesus Christ Who
is the answer, and not only the answer but
the clearly heard answer, to all those griefs.
"This law ordains relief" for the strain and
work of meditation as much as for the great
evil of the world. "This law ordains relief"
for the recluse with his tired eyes strained
against the crucifix. "This law ordains relief
all other law above, that earth cannot contain
its grief." It will come if you let it, it will
cry if you uncover it; you have but to lie
before the all-seeing eye of God, and earth
cannot contain that grief which is its claim ;
"earth cannot contain its grief, nor Heaven
contain its love." And in the moment when
your Holy Week fails, when the Gospel stirs
you not, when the memories of Gethsemane
cannot be reconstructed in the heated theatre
of the brain, when you can no longer ring up
as it were some curtain at your order to the
sacred drama of the Lord's Passion which you
have yourself set upon the stage of fancy ;
when you own yourself hopeless and alone ;
when you say I find nothing but the bare wall
of my cold room, or the emptiness of my poor
cell—then, when there is no person to see but
yourself in your actual place, with your real

grief, with your actual anxiety, with your
trouble about money, with your fretting over
some fault; then when you are yourself and
helpless, and know only your nakedness and
your grief and your futility, or, knowing them
not, let them lie open to the rain and sun of
Jesus Christ's love, then will Christ be present,
not because you have made so fair a shrine of
memory that there needs a vision to complete
the glory of its furniture, but because you are
the sinner for whom He died, and because He
longs still, as at first, to step from Heaven out
of the brightness of the Father's heart into
the nature which He took that He might
redeem it—Himself man, Mediator between
God and man, giving the ransom, fit—not
only sufficient but fit, ἀντίλυτρον—for every
soul ready to have the testimony borne to it
by the spoken voice and by the power of the
Spirit in its own times—such times as this
Week will be if you are content to lie before
the love of God in the helplessness of the grief
which is your claim upon His revelation and
His mercy.

II

TUESDAY IN HOLY WEEK

" Now once in the end of the world hath He appeared
to put away sin by the sacrifice of Himself."—HEBREWS
ix. 26.

IN these short services for busy men we
are obliged to touch in the briefest possible
manner upon subjects which however familiar
would well repay our deliberate and careful
thought. And yet I will spend one or two
of the moments which are open to us in remind-
ing you of what we said yesterday. Just for
this particular effort of our devotion, not in
the least, of course, disparaging other ways
in which you are keeping your Holy Week,
but only for these midday hours of prayer, I
venture to advise you to seek our Lord by
faith according to that abiding reality of His
Heart by which He energizes towards us and
for us in the Passion—to lift up the spirit to
Him by a silent and quiet accepting of the
help of the Holy Ghost rather than by a
strain of memory, or by the most urgent

23

occupation of the imagination and the affections. We are before God now, and He is the same as on that day, and we are the same as those for whom first He died—and so by means of our need and of our nature, by the power of the Holy Ghost, we are able so to make use of the record of the saving actions of the Lord that, holding them as if a golden clue, we come back to His Heart from which those actions proceeded, the Heart which still bends over us, and is willing to communicate to us that richness and that strength by which He died. There is the great reality of the Saviour's Heart, there is the reality of our need. And in our need we have a faculty most fit, most able to arrive at Him, to receive Him. And this faculty which is ours by nature, the faculty of our deep need and poverty, is lifted up by the Holy Ghost into the energy of the redeemed and regenerate life, so that we have to-day, this week, a feature, a part, of that union with Christ in heaven which is the life of the Christian. We are come to the real Mount Sion, to the real Jesus, Mediator of the new covenant. And I will venture once again to remind you that this fact—the mental fact, as you call it —the fact of consciousness, the fact of will, the fact of moral need, the fact of the Saviour's love—this is the deep reality. We are not to

think that by way of a poor substitute for
seeing the sacred wounds in His pierced Side
and Hands and Feet we have the knowledge
of His Heart—as if this were something
offered to grudging acceptance since we cannot again see His pain and grief. No; spirit
is the root of fact. Indeed, that man's mind
is altogether off the track who thinks that
outward things are the model of reality by
which all other existence is to be judged. For
such a man as this it does not greatly matter
whether, by the observation of the world, he
arrives at a positive or a negative conclusion;
for, in fact, his whole mind is rootedly un-
religious, since he supposes that the things
which are seen are the things which govern;
whereas we know that the things which are
unseen are eternal—the things of the mind,
of the heart, of the will, of the purpose. By
this will of the Saviour we are sanctified,
brought into the current of His sacrifice, made
holy; thus, and not otherwise; by the virtue
of His Blood.

So we are not departing from the strictest
and most devout care for the acts of Holy
Week if we resolve to-day in our prayer to
reach after Him, to come to Him, to receive
Him, Who is willing not only to show to us,
but to bestow upon us that powerful energy
of triumphant love which was then, and is

now the true substantial reality of His sacrifice
and death.

And in this thought is a strong consolation
for any who find, as many of us do find,
that the story of the Lord's Passion does not
touch them—does not come home. We are
like thirsty men from whose dry throats the
coolness of the water seems perpetually to
escape. We drink—but there is an elusive
secret of thirst which is not caught and
reached by the tempting draught. Even so,
we hear these words and we know our thirst,
but somehow the Saviour's death in its bitterness cannot sting the palate of our minds.
The story does not reach us—does not pierce
us ; and so it is also in the things we most
deeply care about to-day—and why ? It is,
my brothers, because we have drunk the sorrow
before, because we have known the real bitterness too early. To-day there come to us
in our little home at Oxford personal details
of the plague troubles in Cape Town—of the
people so suddenly struck down that in spite
of organization they lie untended in their
pain ; of a man staggering away from the
doors of the hospital where he could not be
admitted, and hiding himself in the woods.
As it were yesterday, the day before his letter,
Father Congreve was hunting a dying plague
patient who staggered before him through

the copse which covers the rough ground of
our suburbs, and found him and watched by
him there until the health-officer could be
dispatched to relieve his guard.   There is
for the time, among men and women we know
so well, this sense of disorganization, of panic
and disaster.   The terrifying experience of
plague—legendary for us in England—is upon
them at this moment; and we hear it un-
moved.   The children we know lie under its
shadow, the homes we ought to have visited
are visited by the plague-searchers.   Over one
of our own mission-houses floats the yellow
flag.   Among my few Christmas cards is one
from a lad who sickened lately of the strange
disease, and in thirty-six hours was dead.
And yet the terror does not sting us, it does
not pierce—and why ?   Because for years it
has been known—the real bitterness ; the neglect of the poor, the slight regard of human
life, the cruel folly of sanitary neglect.   It has
been known for years—" The first epidemic
that visits us (we used to hear) will sweep off
these people like flies."   Perhaps they are
dying like flies now, and we do not feel it.
Do we not care ?   We care, yes, but it does
not sting us—it does not make the heart beat
faster, it does not make the tears spring—
why ?   Because all the tears are shed.   We
have done all that, we knew that before—we

knew the real thing. The trouble is not that
men should die concomitantly instead of in
series—what does it matter whether they die
by the score this week or die one by one
through the weeks of the year—they have all
to die once, and they none have to die twice.
What is the real tragedy? The real tragedy
is the neglect, the hardness, the selfishness,
the foolishness, the want of providence, the
want of gratitude for God's great gifts. That
is what counts; and we have drunk that cup
and know it. And so when the news comes
to us of divers forms of death, it comes to a
dead heart which has already been beaten
upon till it can sound no more. We are
immune to that poison because we have drunk
of it.

So also when the war came with all its
stories of bloodshed, it did not quicken very
much the pulses of our grief, because we had
known it before. The real substance of it,
the true inwardness of it, the ancient hatred,
the long jealousy, the cruel misunderstandings,
the devilish work of the great enemy himself,
setting brother against brother,—all that had
been done and fixed before ever they went—
strong and wise men—to the council in Bloem-
fontein. That was done and fixed and known
and settled; the blood was shed, whether the
veins were opened or not. And so it is the

real thing, this spiritual and moral fact, the fact of consciousness in us and in God; this is the substantial blessing; this is the substantial curse. And the Lord's Cross and Passion found their reality first in His will, in His Heart, in His Mind, in His love, in His intention and purpose; found their bitterness in the wicked grudge of those who stood about Him, not first in groans and tears and beaded brow. And that reality still stands to-day—the love of God resisted, not accepted; the heart of man hungry and not fed; the poor, fast bound under the heel of the oppressor and not cared for, though God regardeth unrighteousness and wrong from Heaven, and gives His Son to be the poor man for us, to trample under-foot at our peril.

Those are the realities. So we are not substituting something less warm than imagination, something less touching than a picture, something less critically, severely true than the record. On the contrary, we fasten upon the solid reality behind them all, when we offer our naked hearts to God and pray Him to stamp upon them the impression of the Saviour's love, according to the power, according to the system, by means of the guiding points of the actions of which we read.

Now how shall we pursue the study of this

reality? Speaking slowly, as we must in this
vast place, we have now only reached the
beginning. We take first the most familiar
truth. Of our Saviour's death, that which is
most easily said is that it was a sacrifice of
pain. That is the notorious truth concerning
Him—that He was a sufferer and that He
was a sacrifice. To-morrow we will consider
Him as the sufferer—the sinless sufferer—
and so far as time and power permit, ask
what that means. To-day let us consider
Him as our only sacrifice. He gave Himself
to be an offering for sin. He put away sin by
the sacrifice of Himself. The blood of bulls
and goats was typical of His; He came to fulfil
the type—" In burnt offerings and sacrifices
for sin Thou hast no pleasure. Then said I "
—it is the Son of God Who speaks—" lo! I
come to do Thy will, O God." He came to
offer an acceptable sacrifice, and " this Man,
after He had offered one sacrifice for sins for-
ever, sat down on the right Hand of God ;
from henceforth expecting till His enemies be
made His footstool."

We are then to consider His sacrifice—His
glorious and saving sacrifice—the redemption
which comes by the paying down, as it seems to
us, of the Blood.[1] Now this to human hearts—
and it is fortunate, for there are few things more

[1] See Preface, p. vii.

deadening than unanimity—this preaching of the Cross as a blood paid down, as a sufficient and a fit sacrifice and ransom for us, shocks to some extent not only our sense of justice, but that which, believe me, is much nearer to us, our sense of self-regard and human dignity. If you inquire among those who must know the world best whether there is any religious feeling or movement going on amongst those who are not with us in the Church, what there is in the great world which matches to our religion, what kind of thought springs up in real power and motive over there, I believe you will hear this, that the only thing quite clear to our modern is that he must keep himself, that he must make the best of himself, that he must be as the phrase goes, "what he can be." Just as the thrush on the lawn pounces on his proper food, and is so victoriously himself in that, so the man has to be himself. And it is because of this— that he must live his life, that he must be what he is capable of being—because of this and not from any arbitrary dislike for being good, that we must get rid of our Sundays and our worship and our ten commandments; because they check this self-development of the man. That is the new religion, "Keep yourself; live your life; get out of yourself all that you can be. This will which is the real

identity, give it freedom, let it grow, let it
come out; seize what you want. The check-
ing of the desire to take what you want
stunts and falsifies, and tends to nullify that
which is. Never lose your identity. In not
taking what you wish you fail to be what you
are. You are a traitor not to this and that
part of Mosaic morality—you are a traitor
to the deepest interest of your own existence.
For your existence is to will; to manage to
acquire that for which you feel a desire; to
get and to have." What a gospel for the poor!
What a gospel for the *rich!*

Now we, feeling this to have some sort of
sense in it, are obliged to explain the matter
of sacrifice. We are called upon to say that
sacrifice—the sacrifice of the Lord which is
the type and only reality of all sacrifice—is
not destruction, is not the passing away of the
self, is not the crowding down of the feelings,
is not the annulling of the will. Sacrifice
does not consist—that is to say, not char-
acteristically—in death, destruction, abolition,
going out of being. In the ancient ritual it is
not the knife which is characteristic of the
accepted sacrifice. There are offerings in the
Old Testament which have the knife, but
which yet fail of being "most holy." But what
marks the offering which is most holy, most
acceptable, divine, absolutely God's, in ritual

and type and sign ? Why, not the knife, but
the fire. It is the golden flame which wraps
the poor dead offering, takes it up into the
life of Heaven, snatches it out of sight, out of
the waste of life, takes it up into an eternal
continuance—I mean in ritual, symbolically—
into an abiding world. And it is the anti-
type of all this which characterizes sacrifice.
It is the Holy Ghost, the Heavenly Fire
coming down from Heaven, enveloping that
which might have been and now shall not be
wasted because it is taken and accepted into
that golden shroud of the Divine response.
The Holy Ghost, the anti-typal Fire, comes
down and accepts the perfect thing, not spoilt
—just because it is not spoilt—and takes it
up into the secure possession, and the almighty
prevailing power of God, by the merits of
the Lamb to the Throne of love. Even so
He, having offered one sacrifice, was accepted,
and henceforth sits at the right Hand of God,
not as if thus to take back His sacrifice, not
as a way of cancelling His death, but as the
way to live out the life which He truly lived in
the sacrifice, in the passion, in the death. He
comes living to the Father, He offers in victorious might His soul to God, He bursts through
all the bonds, all the snares which keep us
back, and by the Holy Ghost He is strong to
escape, to make His exodus at Jerusalem, to

pass away from our selfishness, to pass away
with us. That is what characterizes sacrifice.
It is the special destiny of the creature that is
offered, not to be lost, but to be kept. What
becomes of the rest of the herd? Do the rest
of the herd live? The cattle upon a thousand
hills are God's, and one is taken for His altar.
Do the rest live? No, the rest die and may
chance to rot upon the plain—as we saw them
three years ago in Africa scattered dead or
buried in their heaps. So the unoffered beasts
of Israel died under the rinderpest in those old
days. That which characterizes the sacrifice
is that out of the herd of Israel all doomed to
death at last, one was taken, preserved by
the salt, accepted by the sanctifying fire,
chosen out and made God's, and symbolically
accepted, as it were, into the sky; taken up
in the cloud of the fragrant smoke to the
presence of God, preserved there, pleading there;
symbolical of the Lord Who, offering Himself
out of our perishing race, taking the nature
which by itself finds itself crumbling to dust
—seized it from us by a strong insistence,
held it all, gripped it firm, pressed it through
all the trials of life, brought it to the place of
rescue, brought it to God, met the responsive
fire of His acceptance, and was taken up
according to the willingness of His sacrifice
into the Heart of God—yes, even in His sacred

creaturely nature—so that, Man with us,
holding us in Himself, one with us, having
our substance—He is preserved by the virtue
of the sacrifice in the eternal peace and power
and life of the Father's Throne—at His right
Hand. That is what is characteristic of sacrifice—not the knife, but the flame. It is the
poor rejected sacrifice which lies there, so
much meat, so much fruit; it is the sacrifice
of the priests of Baal unconsumed ; the sacrifice
of Cain on his unvisited altar. But the
accepted sacrifice is rapt by fire ; and the
sacrifice of the better Abel is translated by
the anti-typal flame of the Holy Ghost. To-
morrow, if it please God, we will try to learn
how it was that this victorious progress which
is the essence of sacrifice—this ebullition of a
life which God had Himself insinuated into
the stream of our human nature—how this
came to suffer, whence the pain came. But
to-day let us only grip this, that the sacrifice
we celebrate, the sacrifice we adore and thank
God for, is a sacrifice of an overflowing life, a
living sacrifice, holy, acceptable unto God—
mounting up by the power of its own will,
welcomed by the living response of the fire
from heaven, of the Holy Ghost into which we
also may enter, for it kindles continually in
the humanity of Jesus, that all the redeemed
may be hidden evermore in the golden fire of

the altar. As blessed Polycarp stood fragrant
within the domed flame of his martyrdom,
so the Church and we in the Church by reason
of our union with Christ may have the kind-
ling spread through us, and by that gorgeous
veil of sacrifice be hid from earthly praise that
we may be accepted up into the continuance
and power of the divine kingdom.

One word more and only one. This sacrifice
is not only the meaning, the inwardness of the
moment of our Lord's passion and death. It
is the meaning of the whole of His Life.
Sacrifice began in His conception; as soon
as He was Man He began to be offered to the
Father. And even if we were to say that it
is earlier than His human life we should but
be using a bold word; for St. Paul tells us
that above in the heavenly counsel there was
already in the mind of the Word Who was to
be Christ—the mind of Christ willing to empty
Himself, to become of no reputation, stooping to
receive us—already this power and will of sacrifice, and why? Because it is the characteristic
of the life of the eternal Word. His life con-
sists in this—the power of a sufficient and a
victorious response to the Father's heart. He
flows out from the Father according to the
power of an unbegun birth—the eternal Sonship; and He flows back to the Father in the
power of an unbegun self-giving—the eternal

Priesthood, perpetually respondent to the
Father's love and invitation. And this, the
eternal characteristic and nature of that stream
of energy which is the life of the Word, as soon
as that Life stepped into our humanity, when
it took up the fragments of our dust, immediately swept them along with the same velocity and in the same direction, with the same
victorious success, up to the Heart of God. A
light chip of wood falls into the rushing
stream. There is no moment during which it
pauses before it picks up the momentum of
the great torrent; but as soon as it touches
the gliding surface of the river, already, at
once, it has the full momentum; already it
sweeps along to the same bourne, at the same
pace, with the same certainty of arrival. And
so when humanity, the light dust of creation,
fell into the broad bosom of the stream of
God's life in the Incarnation, when our nature
as a whole was picked up by the moving
torrent and the responsive glory of the Word,
immediately it was seized upon by the same
law, immediately it sought the same end,
immediately it was impelled to the Father's
Heart at the velocity of Godhead with the
perfection of the Word's eternal and perfectly
sufficient and acceptable love, towards the
Father Who is before all things were, one Life
with the Son and the Spirit in the mystery of

the Godhead. That is the sacrifice of the Lamb. It is the taking up of our nature—or rather it is the falling of our nature with its sorrow and complexity, as it stands, wholly without sin, yet with the sinless consequences of sin, into the broad river, upon the moving mirror of that stream of life which is the eternal Word, Who by reason of His unfaltering love immediately begins to sacrifice it, begins to offer it, holds it up to the Heart of the Father, bends it to the eternal Divine Will, bestows upon it that which is the greatest of all gifts, bestows upon it the glory of acceptance ; gives it the anti-typal acceptation of Abel's offering and Elijah's ; draws down upon it, by the title of His Sonship, by the merit of His virtue, the answering fire of the eternal Spirit. In Christ may we also, trusting to Him, kindled by Him, be taken up an acceptable living sacrifice to the Father, thus proving, finding, knowing in ourselves what is that will of God, wholly good, acceptable and perfect.

III

WEDNESDAY IN HOLY WEEK

" For Christ also hath once suffered for sins, the just
for the unjust, that He might bring us to God, being
put to death in the flesh, but quickened by the Spirit."—
1 PETER iii. 18.

WE promised ourselves yesterday that we
would seek to pursue the thought of our
Lord's sacrifice as an operation of life, of
joyful and successful giving of the self to God,
and inquire how, if it is this, it comes to be
stained with blood and accomplished through
death. Such thoughts appear unpractical to
a certain class of minds; we preach them
because they are such as help our own souls.
It is thus that, in our own experience, some
of us are set more free from theft and envy;
and therefore we think it practical to point
out to sinners the way of the Lord—the story
of Jesus Christ—rather than to rebuke them
in set terms and the briefest sentences for
their daily follies. It becomes very clear
after some years spent in the darkest places

39

of the poor, that what helps a man to walk straight is the knowledge of what Jesus did, and not the echo from the clergyman's throat of the sins which he knows perfectly well before. Pardon me, then, if I cannot accept the suggestion that I ought to talk to you about your sins. I would rather speak to you about your Saviour, and invite you to consider after what inward and most lasting fashion He has saved you; what is the purpose of His Heart and Will; what is the standing reality of His divine and human love.

We saw, then, that sacrifice is an operation of life. It is a success, not a failure; the rising up of the life so as to be given back to God, and therefore saved in the continuance and glory and eternity which belong to God; life which has escaped from the creaturely corruption and found God Who is its Father. If this is so sacrifice answers to creation; it does not answer to judgment, to sin, to Sinai. It answers to creation; we owe it to God because He is our Father. Not because He is our offended Father, but because He is our Father who made us. Since He made us, and so made us that He bestowed upon us a real likeness to His own being, we have this for our success—to return to God; to be yielded and bestowed by an exercise of the will which He gave to us to use. We are

led to take this will, to exercise it; and by
this will—empowered by Jesus Christ—we
also are sanctified by being rendered back
again to God our Father Who made us. And
this follows, we said, from the fact that God
made us in the Word, in Christ, in the Holy
Son, the very form and fashion of Whose
Being is a response to Almighty God, is a
flowing back to the Father's Heart. Therefore we who are made in Christ, in proportion
as we really acquire that community with
Christ in will and thought which is promised
to us by our creation in Him, in proportion as
we enter into His Life, so we enter also into
His sacrifice and are rendered up joyfully and
willingly to God the Father.

But in order to clear this from difficulty,
we have to consider how it is, then, that this
joyful entrance of Jesus Christ in our flesh
into the bosom of the Father, was effected
by the Cross, was stained with mockery and
torture, scourging, spitting, and rejection, by
blood-shedding and by death. And the answer
which we can offer must remain very far from
being complete; nevertheless it may have its
real and practical lesson for us, because it will
teach us and guide us in the answering offering of our own being to God. We shall learn
how to accept in our own Godward life—if it
becomes truly Godward—we shall learn how

to accept the Cross; how to welcome it; how
not to be killed by it; even as our Lord was
not killed by it. For though He was put to
death in the body, He was quickened thereby
in the spirit, and went in that power to preach
to the spirits who long ago had been kept in
chains in darkness in the prison place, since
the unfaithfulness of the time of Noah.

Our answer then is something like this. Our
answer is, the suffering, the Cross, the torture,
the strain, the sweat, the blood-shedding, come
from the circumstance that our Lord was in a
world which hated sacrifice. It was averted
from God. It was different in direction from
that stream moving towards the Father's
Heart which is the Being of the Incarnate
Word. The world was like a rock in the
middle of that stream, breaking the smooth-
ness of its surface, casting it into foam and
anger. The world was hard not because it
was itself a sacrifice, but because it was op-
posed to sacrifice—averted from God's Heart,
willing to keep itself to itself. And so the
Lord when He put Himself in our conditions
—in our nature—and did our work in us,
found the rest of His race opposing the movement of His Heart towards the Father. It
was because our Lord was ready to be offered,
and the world in which He lived had this for
its very note and habit—the desire to keep to

itself what seemed to be its own, the rejection by it of all sacrifice—it was therefore that
our Lord had to burst out from the bonds of
an unoffered humanity, through the gate of
death in order that so He might make His
exodus from an Egypt—a great world-wide
Egypt—through the Red Sea of Passion into
the freedom of the life in God.

Our dear Lord as man, taking our nature
upon Him, took it with all its difficulties; and
He could only wrench it free from its ingrained
selfishness, from the bonds by which men
strive to keep not only themselves but each
other from God, by bursting out through the
gate of death, by presenting His Breast to the
enmity—the age-long enmity—which man has
kept up against God; by going forward in the
love of His Father, in spite of this love rousing
against Him the deepest, the most natural
hatred of fallen man. They hated Him not
because He was great, or clever, or beautiful,
or beloved. They hated Him because they
knew not either Him or His Father. They
hated Him for His godliness, because His life
was a stream set steadily towards God. Therefore it necessarily came into conflict with the
world, which had this for its principle of
preservation—to keep God at arm's length;
to render Him a bull or goat, if so it might
be, but by all means to avoid rendering the

will, the soul, the heart, the life, back to the
Father Who had made them. This our Lord
Himself teaches us. They hated Him because
they had not known either Him or His Father.
They did not know the Sonship in Him which
bore Him steadily to the Father's Heart.
They did not know the love of the Father,
drawing Him up into that home of rest. And
so all His movements were hateful to them
and His life was so essentially in contradiction
to the whole current of their work, that it led
Him to this surfing place—this breach of the
waters—this breaking out of death, because
of the impact of two great moral forces ; for
the force of the Incarnate Word, raising the
created humanity in obedience to the Father,
met the force of the fallen nature of man
steadily turning away from God, refusing to
assent, straining to keep its own mind, its
own doings, to itself. To hold together and
to keep themselves close—that is the desire of
mankind ; and He Who ascends towards God
must face the enmity of the Cross.

This may teach us something—very little,
but still something—of the reason why our
Lord's joyful sacrifice was stained on our side
with the indignity of blood. He came on
account of sins—περὶ ἁμαρτιῶν. The word
is used in the most general possible sense.
Somehow, "because of sins," because of the

estrangement of human nature, the Godward life set in our midst became necessarily the crucified life. But it redeemed our fallen nature by its own Godward trend ; and only because of the life's Godward movement was the Cross which is our share in it made holy and redeeming and good. It was the holy sacrifice which sanctified that altar, the altar which, as we set it up, had no title to receive in any way the regard of God.

Let us consider a little further if we may, and in terms of our modern daily life which I cannot think will give any sensible man offence, this estrangement of men from God as it has always been and is now. It is an estrangement, a degradation, a falling to pieces of society, which in one aspect, from one point of view, may be spoken of as the result of our solitude—the result of our separation from God. We are told by those who know the world in distant places, that in small communities where men are shut up year after year in a solitary station, in the midst of the wilds, with only a few to deal with—we are told by a well-known writer to remember, even if we cannot understand it—"that all laws weaken in a small and hidden community where there is no public opinion." Now I will be so bold as to say that our human evil is nothing else but this

" station " evil, written out large. What is
the evil of the frontier station in India is
when written large the evil of the whole of
Humanity—because we lack our public, which
is God.   There is but one public for us to live
to; there is but one eye under which we can
construct anything which can be called a conduct.   And for lack of this public, for lack of
this eye under which the true life of man
must always be lived, for lack of the public
opinion of Heaven, which is God, our whole
society went long ago to pieces, simply because
we were shut up, creature with creature, in a
limited number, bound down to all the penury
of our bankrupt condition; for we had lost
the riches God meant us to administer.   In
this state, with our poor character, with our
lack of knowledge, and above all things with
the want of an eye which we could really
appeal to, a heart towards which we could
really pour out our life—because of this it
was (in one way, this is one aspect of it)
that we went to pieces at the first, and go
to pieces still.   We are a solitary, segregated
community of people, unless we have God.
It is God alone—the Eye of God, the
Thought of God, the Heart of God, the
Face of God—it is this alone—nothing else
will do and nothing less—which keeps any
one of the offices round about us in St. Paul's

Churchyard honest. It is this alone which makes it worth while to add up our columns fitly, to take our place aright, to be faithful to our wives, to go on with our work, to search our consciences, to get out our sins. It is the Eye of God alone, the Love of God alone, which draws out anything which is in the least good in the nature which He has created. Its whole being is to go back to Him. He is the air in which it lives, even as this air we breathe is the very substance of the plants which flower so brilliantly in it. So also we can live only in the Heart of God. And apart from that, hidden from that, immediately our society, our life, our conduct, our mind, suffer eclipse, degradation, disorganization, sin and death. Now into this society, this disorganization, this disgrace, this helplessness, came the Lord Jesus with His Eye upon the Father; and He walked amongst us before that Face; He led amongst us the Godward life, and He cured us by this. He suffered, the just for the unjust, in the matter of sins, to bring us to God; bore up, by the power of His will, by the patience of His love, bore up the creation which we had degraded, and sanctified it by holding it in this light of the Divine presence which is its life and purity. "If we walk in the light as He is in the light," says St. John, teaching

just this lesson, " we have fellowship one with
the other, and the Blood of Jesus His Son ,
cleanseth us from all sin." And that which
is the law of our obtaining pardon by His
Blood is the law also by which He established
the pardon at the first. It was a pardoning
effected by light. It was the bringing of the
creature into the glory of God—bringing us
out of darkness into the liberty of the glory
of the children of God. It was the Lord
with His Eye upon the true public, the true
object of worship, the true object of desire,
the true Judge, the true Father. It was He
Who taking our nature by a real discipline,
by a genuine effort, kept it up there, so that
He, sanctifying it in the piece, laid open a
door by which we all, through the Blood of
Jesus, might also enter into the holiest place,
might come into the light, might be redeemed
from the disorder, from the hatred, from the
sin, from the lust which is in the world
through the corruption and falling to pieces
still caused by our departure from the
Face of God our Father. That is sacrifice
triumphant through suffering, bursting its
way out by blood because we resisted His
passage and dragged back the captain of our
salvation, Who would lead us across the river
of death into the freedom of a new life. He
has to burst from us and, pursued by our

curses, works out the salvation that we need. And then, more particularly, our evil is set forth in the Bible under an expression which is much more than a figure, and which is a fact of to-day, a fact no doubt fit to shock the ears of the polite ; the fact, I mean, of the difference between rich and poor. That fact in the Bible is not a mere example, a mere touch; one thing among many with which God finds fault, with which God is displeased. Nay, that difference between the rich and the poor is the very poison, the very wound, the very disgrace from which we suffer. All through the Old Testament there goes that cry—God has taken upon Him the cause of the poor and the oppressed. That is the essence of sin, the making of rich and poor. For at the root of sin, the deepest thing in sin, is covetousness ; the desire to keep back to one's self what belongs to God, and belonging to God, is to be used by all the brethren in their turn, in their place, according to their need ; the setting up of another title besides necessity for the use of the fruits of the earth. That is the root crime of mankind, covetousness. And from this covetousness, and the cruel division which it makes, spring all our evils. Every form of lust is covetousness, selfish desire ; the desire of the neighbour's house ; the desire of the neighbour's goods ;

the desire of the neighbour's wife. The great
division between those who seize and those
who lose runs through all life. It is not a
division merely of class, of the great and
the simple, of the high and the low. It is
the old division of the rich and the poor;
the old cause of murder; the old tragedy
of Cain and Abel. It is the contrast between the receiver and the thief. It is the
contrast between the procuress and the poor
lass whom she drags down to hell. It is the
great division of mankind. There is none
so deep as that. Alas! too often it is the
division between white and black. It is the
great deep-rooted division between the men
who have, and hold, and seize, and covet, and
will keep for themselves, and those who ask
only to be allowed to live and who cry out
to God; between those who have need of
nothing, and those others, " the hungry, which
make oil within our walls, and tread our
winepresses and suffer thirst " (Job xxiv. 10,
11). The poor oppressed man—the whole
Old Testament is full of his cry, and all the
Psalms. " When God maketh inquisition for
blood," what does He ask for ? " He forgetteth
not the complaint of the poor." When God's
time for remembrance comes, what is it that
He regards ? " The poor shall not always be
forgotten, the patient abiding of the meek

shall not perish for ever." The words are all
on one page of our Prayer Book. When the
ungodly stirs up his lust, who is his object?
"The ungodly for his own lust doth persecute
the poor"; whether it be the ignorant or the
noble or the beautiful, or those who have no
money or those who have no friends. The
ungodly makes boast, of what? Of his
crime, of his drunkenness? No; of having
his own way; his own "heart's desire." And
so the cry all through is, "Arise, O Lord God,
and lift up Thine hand; forget not"—what?
"Forget not the poor." "Come that Thou
mightest take the matter into Thine Hand.
The poor committeth himself unto Thee for
Thou art the Helper of the friendless. Lord
Thou hast heard the desire of the poor, Thou
preparest Thine heart and Thine ear hearkeneth
thereto, to help the fatherless and the poor
unto their right that the man of the earth be
no more exalted against them."

Now I would say to you, dear brethren, if
you look round for some way to understand
the Lord's Passion, and find you cannot grasp
it; if you reject as fanciful, or too thinly spun,
the kind of thoughts which I have suggested
concerning the inward reason of His death,
take this for your lesson which every man
may grasp. Jesus Christ died—why? Because He was poor; because He had not

enough money; because He had not enough
friends; because He was not chosen, but
rejected. That is why He died; that is how
it was possible; that is how it came to pass.
There were deeper things. It was the will of
the Lord putting in His light into our fallen
world. It was the joy of the Redeemer rising
up through our rending nature to God the
Father Who was His Home. But in the
nearest possible aspect, in the baldest and
simplest, and yet quite a true sense, you may
say He died because He was on that side of
the fence, not on this. He belonged to the
helpless; He belonged to the poor; He stood
where the dark-skinned people stand to-day;
He stood where the ragged people stand to-
day; where the ignorant stand to-day; where
the friendless stand to-day. Had He been a
rich man, had He been a noble, had He been
a Roman like St. Paul, we do not know in
what manner He could have accomplished
His Passion. And poverty we know to be a
fundamental character of His work, part of
His genuine object, essential to His method
of salvation. For we are told that up in
Heaven, when His mind stirred to take upon
Him our case, He willed not only to empty
Himself, but to take upon Himself the form of
a slave and to be made in the fashion of a poor
man that He might be obedient unto death,

even the death of a slave, the death of the
Cross. That division, the division of those
who have and those who have not, runs so
deep as almost to run to the bottom, and you
may say that it is one account of the Saviour's
death, that now at last the long groaning
which we hear through the Old Testament
finds its answer. And how? The poor cried
out, "Lord remember the poor who committeth his case unto Thee"; the poor of
every station, from the highest poor man, the
poor man with a crown who is rejected by his
people, to the lowest poor man with the bare
feet just driven from his door, the wanderers
who "are wet with the showers of the mountains, and embrace the rock for want of a
shelter" (Job xxiv. 8). All these alike cry out
to the Lord, "Lord remember the poor—the
poor committeth his cause unto Thee." And
what is the answer of the Lord God—the
King of kings, the Sovereign, the Almighty,
the Ever Rich? He so accepts their cause as
not to carry it as the Roman, by his legal
standing, carried his client's plea; not to carry
it as our friends take our cause into their
hands to hand it on with their good-will, with
all the power of their influence. But He so
accepted it as to make it His own. He
clothed Himself in the naked flesh; He
covered Himself with the disgraced habit; He

wore the face of sorrows and was sheltered in the station of contempt. He so accepted the cause of the poor for all ages and for ever up to the last day. There is no poor man, from the poor Christian native in China to the poor unbelieving Englishman who cannot manage to hear the Creed he desires to know, who has not Jesus specially for his brother; for He has so accepted the cause of the poor as to make it His own in His very Person. The cry has gone up, and the old contrast—between the poor man crying to God and God looking down upon the poor—this division between God and the poor has been done away. Age after age the poor stood there before the face of God begging for relief, begging for deliverance from the oppressor. And behold God has leaped the gulf, that great gulf which unless we bridge it now will be found fixed between us and the poor man in Abraham's bosom. While the rich are still hesitating to cross the stream to where the poor lie, God has leaped down out of His Royal throne and made so great a junction between the two that the oppressed and their Avenger are one. The Lord Who should visit—the Lord Whose eyes behold iniquity and search it out—those eyes like a flame of fire; the Lord Who forgetteth not the poor has taken upon Him their cause, and is their own, and is one of

themselves. So that now the poor are avenged
by having God in their midst. And by this
we are not to think that the Lord has so
taken their cause as to take the inability of
the poor man; but rather we are to think that
the oppressed is so lifted up as to hold in his
bosom the dignity of divine justice. There in
the rags is the community with Jesus. There
in the oppressed, high and low—in the mis-
understood, in the blamed, in the cursed—
there in those who bear our scorn, is the
special community of Jesus. Can we ask
then why He suffered? Do not *they* suffer?
Can we ask then why He was kept on the
rack? Are *they* allowed to slumber at their
ease, to take their rest in peace? Can we ask
why He had no place to lay His Head? Have
all the poor their mansions ready for them?
In your London have you replaced the streets
you are obliged to pull down? Do you take
care for the poor as the Lord does? I am
speaking, I know, to the poor, but I must
speak to those who are not poor also. Why
should we wonder that Jesus shed His blood?
Do not *they* shed their blood for us? Why
should we wonder that His sweat was dark
like gore? Have you never heard of their
sweat and their pain? Of their tears, of their
disappointments, of their dangers, of how
their daughters are entrapped, of how their

children run to waste, of how their young
men lie as it were groaning in all our streets?
Why should our salvation be without tears
when it is so long a time yet till the "streets
of our city shall be full of boys and girls play-
ing" (Zech. viii. 5); full of children praising
God? If there is pain in your London, do
not be surprised that there is pain in your
Saviour, for He has taken upon Him the cause
of London, the cause of "the poor who faint
alway," of the multitudes, of the sick, of the
despised, of the rejected, of the sinful, of
those we call the fallen, of those who are on
the pavement or off the pavement, of those
whom we drag through the mud which is the
wretched accretion of our wheels of commerce.
He has taken their cause, and until they cease
from sobbing before the ears of the Most
High, until there is "no complaining in our
streets," no anguish in our great Empire, till
that day comes we ought not to be looking
for a key by which to open the lock of the
secret of the Saviour's suffering—Who when
He came to be holy and meek and just in
our midst, leaped the great gulf and clothed
Himself in the person of those whose cause
He came for ever to avenge; to avenge not
by anger and strife and blood, but by pity and
by bearing them in His bosom into the home
of the eternal Father, where by the prayers of

Lazarus who lies outside our gates may we, through His great mercy, and through a sufficient repentance at last, find some lowly place, if it be but in the poorest quarter of the Heavenly City.

NOTE.—The passages about our divine Saviour's deep and actual community of life with the poor of this world might bear—as my dearest friend shows me—a false meaning. I think they are patient of a true one, and I leave them nearly as they stand in the shorthand. I did not and do not mean that our Lord suffered or was condemned or hated *for being poor*. He was condemned on a charge of treason-blasphemy, and was hated for His actual conflict with the received religious practice of a fallen Church. But His poverty co-operated as an actual cause of His Passion. If Judas had been the paid follower of a rich man he would not have been tempted; had the Saviour been of those who have, a Herodian, a Cæsarian, "one of the rulers," could His end have taken the same course? Had He been, like Paul, a Roman, He would not have endured the Cross. These things, accidental to a certain form of judgment, are not without substantial significance Doubtless His poverty was not the determining cause of our Lord's suffering. Doubtless also it was not for nothing that the road by which He actually passed to the Cross was the road of the poor.

IV

THURSDAY IN HOLY WEEK

"So after He had washed their feet, and had taken His garments, and was set down again, He said unto them, Know ye what I have done to you? Ye call Me Master and Lord : and ye say well; for so I am. If I then, your Lord and Master, have washed your feet ; ye also ought to wash one another's feet. For I have given you an example, that ye should do as I have done to you."—St. John xiii. 12–15.

And earlier :

"What I do thou knowest not now; but thou shalt know hereafter."—St. John xiii. 7.

We see that our Lord, willing that His people should know the meaning of His Passion, invites them to learn through actions which we call common ; speaks to them in terms which sound to our ignorance, below the level of mystery or revelation ; gives them an example of service for their imitation. By action in what we suppose the unsupernatural sphere of conduct, He will lead them to know what it is that He does for them in things past finding out; what

is the great and unsearchable mystery of our
redemption by His Passion and Death. He
will show them through the common thing,
through the moral conformity which seems to
us within the scope of nature, according to the
law of charity and through the obedience of
kindness. Thus by imitation they shall come
to know what in inward truth He does. "What
I do thou knowest not now"—either in this
action or in any of the great actions of Holy
Week. "But thou shall know hereafter, for
I have given you an example, that ye should do
as I have done to you." It is His word to St.
Peter, who looking back in the meekness which
we hear in his first epistle transmits the lesson
to us—"He left you an example that ye should
follow His steps" (1 Peter ii. 21). And so
yesterday we seemed to see that to us, separated
by so long a history, as we search to know the
mystery of Christ crucified for us, there comes to
greet and to help us the common mystery, the
universal fact of pain and loss. Pain and sorrow
help us to climb to Him by the two approaches
of pity and of patience. The pain we bear
joins us to our Lord when He bestows on us
His gift of patience. The pain we witness is a
link to Him through His real community with
the suffering, and calls for the pity through
which we minister to Him in them. By this
double access we may come into the law of His

Being, and even know in part how it fared with Him when He hung for us upon the Cross, deserted by men, hidden from the Face of God. By pity and by patience we come. Christ has died for us ; therefore we are to be loving, tender-hearted, pitiful one to the other— "forgiving one another even as God, for Christ's sake, hath forgiven" us. Christ has offered Himself as sacrifice for sins once. Therefore we are to have patience, in conformity and communion, because "Christ also suffered for sins once, the just for the unjust, to bring us to God." And we are wise if we know that this following of His example, this patience under pain, this pity towards the weak, are not merely accessories of the central mystery ; but that, because in God is nothing unnecessary, nothing unmeaning, there lies in these things ready for our grasp, the very mystery of His redeeming love. And in truth we have in our Holy Week no surer access to the Lord, than by the way of penitence for sins, and by the way of pity and of patience in face of sufferings, patience in our own sufferings—pity for the sufferings of the neighbour. And this great truth, that spiritual access to our Lord is secured by the following of His example according to His word (as when He said, "If any man will come after Me, let him take up his cross daily and follow Me"), all this is put before us in two great significant actions to-day, the sacrament of the Holy Eucharist and the Maundy—the Lord's command—the duty of the feet-washing. In these two ways, communion and charity, by a substantial communication with Jesus Christ, we are to be held up firmly into the healing truth of the precious Blood. Let us consider them in turn.

First, the Maundy and then the Eucharist. Our Lord did the Maundy that we might know what He was, what He would have us to do, what is the mystery of His Passion and of our salvation. It is a mystery of charity, it belongs to the law which is so familiar to us, so hard to fulfil, the duty of giving out of our store, of bearing the burden of the weak. And we are to notice that He comes to it in His Majesty, as our Lord and Master. When He stoops, He reminds His disciples of His greatness—" Ye call me Master and Lord and ye say well for so I am." He girded Himself for the work because, St. John says, "He knew that He came forth from God and goeth again to God." It was because of the dignity of His Divine origin, it was because of the prospect of the eternal glory with which He would clothe our humanity in His Person, it was on the eve of His exaltation that He now seemed, to our sense, to stoop—rose from supper, left the feeding; made Himself a minister, sat no longer

to be served ; girded Himself with the towel,
took water and washed all their feet in turn,
yea, even the feet of Judas into whose heart
Satan had already shot the arrow of treachery.
Right through to the end went the feet-washing,
done by our Lord, in the special consciousness
(may we dare to say), at any rate in the special
revelation of the glory of His Divine prerogative
and home, because He came forth from the
Father and returneth to the Father.   Knowing
all this, He loved His own unto the end, and
girded Himself, and took water and washed,
saying to them, "I am your Lord and Master,
ye call me so, and ye do well, for so I am."   So
He stooped ; but He stooped in His Majesty ;
and it is well for us to remember this.   For we
lose in part the benefit of His humility, if we
think of it as some passing eclipse of the real
and essential greatness of Christ.   We are not
to think of His Passion and Death, of the
mocking and His silence, of His scourging and
His imprisonment, as we think of the indig-
nities which we put, for example, upon our
King in the great Revolution three centuries
ago.   We are not to think of them as the
partial and temporary obscuring of a sover-
eignty which will presently emerge and reassert
itself.   Nay, these things—this humiliation,
this lowliness, this poverty—these are the glory
of God.   This is how man must be when God

is in his heart. This is the reversal of our disgrace. He was poor in order that by His poverty the stain of our gold might be wiped off from the face of man, the yellow dust no longer disfigure the brow created for a heavenly crown of love. Even so

> " Wrath by His meekness,
> And by His health sickness,
> Are driven away
> From our immortal day." [1]

This poverty, this emptiness, this lowliness, this obedience, this ministration, these are the marks of Him who is greatest of all. " Let him who is the greatest among you be your minister." Here is His exaltation, here is the throne of God's glory when it sets itself among men.

So this was no evil thing to be reversed, this was no stripping to be again clothed upon; but in this humility, in this sacrifice, in this bearing of the burden of others, Jesus asserted His unity of being with God, Who is always the poor man of the world, who does not keep one sparrow's feather for His own, who reserves in the unsearchable glades of Heaven no spot exclusively for Himself; the Lord God, who is as some great King, who has thrown open all His crown lands to be trodden under foot of man and who, in the wide reaches even of unimaginable existence, has nothing so for His

[1] William Blake, *Night.*

own that it shall not belong to all men if they
will come to Him.   God the great pauper, God
the poor man, shows the unity of Jesus with
Himself, by making Him on the earth altogether
nothing—do service, bear humiliation, be despised. This is the glory of the Lord's eternal
riches, battling against the false riches which
are poverty—those scramblings and scratchings
together of the perishing things of this world,
which are the very mark of the penury of our
spiritual existence.

And so, let us understand it, the stooping is
not something to be reversed, the stooping lies
in the road of His exaltation. "Now is the
Son of Man glorified, and God is glorified in
Him."   And accordingly when He was seen of
one again in Heaven, when St. John fell at His
feet as dead, and then looked up in answer to
the merciful voice, he saw the same Lord in
His transfiguration, still "girded about the paps
with a golden girdle," the transfigured symbol
of the service which He has made eternally
His own, the girdle of a priest, the girdle of a
minister, the golden girdle, mark of a service
which He has put next His heart. Round the
breast, close to His heart, lies the mark of a
perpetual servitude and ministry to all His
brethren.

That is the feet-washing. It is not some
defeat of the Lord's majesty which must pre-

sently be redressed, but it is the exhibition of
the law of His greatness, of the power of His
salvation, an exhibition of that which has a
short name we know well, the name of Love.
It invites us to contemplate the eternal victory
and divine nature of love. "No man hath
seen God at any time," but if he loves the
brethren—loves them not in word but in deed,
in service and in feet-washing—he shall know
God ; for "he that dwelleth in love dwelleth
in God."

And then, on the other hand, the Lord Jesus,
showing us this mystery of service, shows us
also the mystery of offering to God. He gives
us the Holy Eucharist, the communication of
His sacred humanity. He gives us herein
the power of His Body and His Blood, He
makes us become men as He was Man, He
draws our hearts to be hearts like His human
Heart, He would have our blood pulse with the
loving-kindness which was in His blood—His
life. This is the Holy Eucharist. Sweeping
aside all difficulties by which Christians are
divided, here, let us say, in this holy mystery,
the Lord Jesus bestows upon us substantially
the real power, the real communication of His
sacred human nature, God-filled with might
and with love. But even in this mystery,
which is thus primarily a mystery of our feeding
by God, of the giving to us of that which was

E

not our own, even here is the note of tenderness one to another, of brotherly love. Even here, down to the smallest details—"Take ye this and divide it among yourselves." "Drink ye all of you of this." So far does this principle of community and of brotherliness extend, that it regards the minor morals of courtesy. And later, but still in the Church's first age, there is St. Paul to teach, "When ye come to the Lord's Table wait one for the other, be careful of each other's feelings, shame not those that have not houses to eat and drink in, preserve a seemly order, see that all take their places—wait ye one for another." Even in these lesser things we ought to see no mere decoration or useless fringe of the gospel mystery, but the will of the Lord of Love coming out there, holding fast there in the quiet manners of daily life, the important details of true Christian ceremonial. For what is the true ceremonial of the Altar ?

The ceremonial of brotherly courtesy, and gentle consideration ; of waiting one for another ; of seeing that no man is offended, no man shamed, no man abashed, no man taken out of his depth, no man hindered in his walk to the Lord's Table ; but every one welcomed, every one guided, every one comforted, every one consoled. In the care for the poor, for the ignorant, and in consideration for those who

differ from us; there are most fit adornments
and worthy accessories of the great mystery of
the Lord's Sacrifice. And from His feeding of
our poor souls—linked with the mystery, the
truth about brotherly love, about courtesy to
the poor—we go on further to see that this
feeding which we receive as one family, as
one body, in the orderliness of authority and
courtesy and tenderness,—this feast of the
Body and Blood of the Lord is the eternal
offering; is that One Body by which we are
sanctified—is that which He offered through
the Holy Ghost once for all. And in this Gift
we also are offered; not only mysteriously, as
men say—not only by some transference unseen of our being and life into the Life and
Being of Jesus, given in an unknown fashion
to us—but also in the active sacrifice of daily
choice. This is a part of the truth of the
eternal sacrifice, of the eternal sacrifice in
Heaven, and of our coming up into it by the
Holy Eucharist. Yet we somewhat miss that
more prosaic meaning of the Eucharistic sacrifice which is so particularly characteristic of
St. Augustine, the truth that we also, if we
will, if we are good, if we are penitent, if we
are loving, lie there upon the Altar, joined
there into the bread and wine which are
offered—the whole congregation and the separate individuals—to the Lord in a glorious

community with Jesus in the very heart of His Life, that Life which is the taking up of humanity into the Father's acceptance. There in the supreme moment of the redemptive life we can be joined in, we can pass on, we can reach home by the way which has been opened to us and sanctified through the veil, the Way that is His Flesh. We also, having a High Priest, enter in with spiritual sacrifices, with the gift of heart and life and worship and hope, all filled and nourished by this same God-filled humanity; we also get home by the road of love and sacrifice to the eternal Heart.

And upon that thought I would add two words. First this: our sacrifice, our love to Christ, our wish to belong to Him, can never be true, our acceptance in Him can never be sure, our washing by the precious Blood can never quite convince us, unless it comes out through the charity of which we spoke—unless it comes out through the offering which we make of ourselves to God. On the one hand washing, cleansing, good-conduct, peace of mind are given through the sacrifice. On the other hand the sacrifice seizes us and holds us through confession of sins, through abandonment of faults, through love of the neighbour.

The mystery must run both ways. We must strive to reach Jesus through the real

acknowledgment of our faults. But we shall
only find true confession through the real
accepting of Christ. First, we must know
the Precious Blood of which this week speaks,
by the true utterance of our sins; and if
there is any whom we have wronged, here
we have within our grasp the act we need.
Or if we have wronged the Church and fallen
away gravely from the law of Christian life,
we owe something to the Church, we owe the
Church truth. We must seek of God, we
must pray God by His Holy Spirit to show us
how we may pay what we owe to the brotherhood—to the body in which God has set us.
Not as something additional and insignificant,
but as the very sacrament of our life in Christ,
we must have peace in the body. For it was
unto this peace we were called when we were
called unto Jesus Christ Himself. So there is
one thing. If we desire to know Him, to
inherit His Blood, to be surely saved by Him,
we must see that by action we arrive at Him,
claim Him, seize hold of Him. But on the
other hand—and this seems to me more practically important—on the other hand we shall
never arrive at good actions, we shall never
arrive at good honest charity, we shall never
attain to true confession and real restitution,
excepting by that sacrifice of Jesus Christ
accepted. If on the one hand true community

with Christ requires the obedience of a life,
how much more deeply, and at the same time,
how much more immediately important it is
to remember that we shall never arrive at a
good life excepting by the mercy of Christ
accepted by us as we are, by praying to
Christ to take us that we may be offered
to the Eternal Father.

My second practical word is this. That
thought of an offering to the Father means to
those who know their own hearts a most real
advance in the art of holy living, in the art of
holy prayer. In a life of grace you may perhaps mark these three stages. There is at
first the state of the man, who tries to be good
in order that he may reach Christ ; to make
his soul right, that afterwards he may become religious. He is in the Old Testament
state and strives to conquer sin as a prelimi-
nary to receiving the mercy of God. He
is already arrived at the track, but alas! he
makes no progress along it, he stands beat-
ing at the wicket. And the second stage is
reached when men understand that they are to
receive from God all the benefit that God has
given us by His only-begotten Son, born and
crucified and risen again, and that all we have
to do is continually to keep the heart open,
that this rain of Divine grace which is Jesus
Christ, may enter in and change and lift us

up, cleansing us and making us strong in a
life of righteousness. That is the great second
stage, when we understand that long before
our penitence, even while we were yet sinners,
Christ died for the ungodly, and that there is
now no condemnation for them that are in
Christ Jesus, who will accept Him, who will
take the offer, who will open the heart, who
will enter by the Holy Ghost into this mystery
of " Christ in us, the hope of glory." The
coming in, the visit of Jesus, the pouring
down of the Holy Ghost; that is the second
stage of a life of grace. Now the man begins
to make progress, now he continually renews
his struggle, and now day by day, however
little he knows it, he has his victories, or God
wins true victories in him. But there is a
third stage which comes to us after disappointment, comes to us when we have found
how often we lapse from the memory of
Christ, how often we close our hearts against
the incoming of the Holy Ghost, how often
we fail to look in and visit that mystery in us
—" Christ in us, the hope of glory "; how
little we know by daily experience that Christ
is in us of a truth. When we begin to
tremble and fear lest after all we be reprobate
and have lost Him, then God encourages us,
and recovers us by the invitation to remember
a still higher way to Him, if it may be so

called, the way, that is to say, of offering
oneself soul and body to enter into God
instead of striving only to open the narrow
heart that God may enter in. And because
the road in God is wide and open, because the
Heart of Jesus, which is the wicket, is so great
that no man may miss it; because this way
is victorious and sanctified by the Blood of
Jesus, a way made open to the heavenly place,
therefore we do in fact find that the man who
thus frames in his thought the fashion of his
approach to God finds it more secure, finds it
more constant, finds it so that even in his
worst mood he does not err therein. In his
moods, in his darkness, in his impenitence as
he calls it, in his grief and pride; he feels as
if a veil were between him and God. There
can be, he feels, no entrance, and he must
wait until Christ pierces the veil of sin and
grief, to enter in once more. He cries out to
Him to visit his soul.

"Dark and cheerless," he cries—

> "Dark and cheerless is the morn
>   Unaccompanied by Thee;
> Joyless is the day's return,
>   Till Thy mercy's beams I see;
> Till they inward light impart,
> Glad my eyes, and warm my heart."

"Visit then," he prays—

" Visit then this soul of mine,
    Pierce the gloom of sin and grief,
Fill me, Radiancy Divine,
    Scatter all my unbelief;
More and more Thyself display,
    Shining to the perfect day."

And it is an appealing cry to God; it goes
to His Heart, and it springs naturally from
ours. But it is not always ours. There is a
time when the heart cannot even cry out for
Christ to come. There is a time when the
door at which He knocks seems bolted, or
as if we had lost the passage which leads
to it, so that we cannot open it to admit
the Guest we long for. And at such times,
when we are dead and dry, when we grope
in the corridors of our dark house of life, and
cannot find the key of consciousness to let
the true Light in, then opens out this other
way; there shines the broad path of Christ's
Heart. Then we remember the great word
which answers that in which He has said to
us, " Behold, I stand at the door and knock;
if any man hear My voice, and open the door,
I will come in unto him." We remember
there is another word, " Knock and it shall
be opened." There is the heart of Jesus waiting to let us in. There lies the road of sacrifice broad and shining before us—" the path
of the just that shineth more and more unto
the perfect day." And those among us, those

among you, dear brethren, who know your
own hearts, will bear me out if I say that in
our darkest gloom, in our worst mood, in our
most obstinate impenitence as it seems, we
can yet rise up, we can still offer ourselves as
we are to God, that He may take us in Jesus
Christ and disentangle the confused motives
and rescue the treasure which lies hid, and
purge away the dross that encumbers and
make us truly His own, as we offer effort and
love, or hatred or pain or despair to God, in a
mass with our best hopes and our best desires,
through Jesus Christ, Who has gone before us
to show us a path. He took our human nature,
and with it trod up to God through the
way of the Cross, opening for us a gate into
the most holy way which is His flesh, that
we also, because we have a High Priest,
should thus in Him come boldly to the Throne
of Grace, offering ourselves, body, soul and
spirit, a sacrifice, willing and loving and acceptable to God, which is our reasonable
service, our spiritual liturgy, our effectual
union with Jesus Christ, crucified for us and
living for ever for us, in us, we in Him, in the
Heavenly places.

GOOD FRIDAY

INTRODUCTORY

My Brethren, I believe we shall best
husband our time if we spend at first more
than a few moments in making the nature of
our Devotion clear to ourselves. The work
before us is a work of prayer. We claim this
sacred Three Hours, a space in which to yield
ourselves with special love and trust to the
care of God; in which to receive a real share
in the sacred memories of the Passion. By
the Power of the Holy Ghost—"in the Spirit"
—we seek to know Jesus according to the
mystery of His suffering obedience even unto
death, the death of the Cross. And in this
search our object is not past and distant, but
actual and near. We do not attempt so to
stir our fancies and emotion as to make that
appear to be present, which is not present in
fact. But, praying in the Holy Ghost, keeping
ourselves in the love of God, we hope by
God's mercy really to arrive, in the true life of

75

the soul, at real facts which are really waiting
for our faith to-day.

Let us consider what are the great realities
which belong as much to us and to this day as
they belong to the day of our Divine Saviour's
Passion. Is there any abiding fact which is
common to the two days and links them
securely together, making our watch as sacred
as the hours when Mary stood with John
beside the Cross—facts of to-day which were
facts on the morning of the saving Death, and
have not changed? It is by these we shall
make our approach, and not by seeking to
imagine, as if in dramatic representation, that
our Lord is crucified afresh. Rather, we know,
the very foundation of true prayer is the ador-
ation of our Lord as He is in Heaven. "As
for our God He is in Heaven, He hath done
whatsoever pleased Him." We are to lift up
our hearts to Jesus Christ, near to us, at the
right hand of the Father in unspeakable bliss
and glory and power.

But so seeking, we have two realities to-
day in common with that past day of the
Passion. The first of them—the nearest of
them to us in some sense—is our own sin
and grief and weakness; and, related to
these, the disorder, the evil, the sadness
that are in the world round about us, and
the failure that is even in the Holy Church

in its earthly members. There is that great reality of sin, of sorrow, of pain, of grief, of emptiness, the same to-day as it was upon the day that our Lord suffered; the world is truly lying before Him, needing His help to-day as then, still full of darkness and cruel habitations. Each generation is born in sin; the work of salvation has to be done afresh within the space of each man's life. A Christian ancestry in the order of nature does not avail to lighten that curse. Every man as he comes into the world comes with the same need of God as the first fallen man; comes with the entire inability to cure his evil, to reach to the Eternal Life. That is the first great reality of to-day; the reality of evil, in ourselves, in the world, in the Church; the reality of the sinner's guilt and the sinner's need.

And over against this is an answering reality—the Heart, the Love of Jesus Christ, our Lord, God and Man, "The same yesterday, and to-day, and for ever." He waits for us, near to us, nearer to us than our own frame and circumstances; nearer than the neighbour by our side—"nearer to us than breathing, and closer than hands and feet"—yet at the right hand of the Father. He waits for us, strong and constant, and having in His heart still the true reality of His Passion, its moral fountain; that from which all His suffering, all His obedience sprang, the Mind of Christ Jesus, the pity for the sinner, the loyalty to the Father, the willingness to undergo the Cross, even unto the Death—all this is in Him still in the unchangeable constancy of His Heart, which is a human Heart taken up into the power of Divine Life, accepted and made part of the perpetual property and attributes of God. And yet this Heart, though constant and unchanging, has in it movement, variety, life for all our needs. Though it stands there constant and the same, pouring out like a fountain the unfailing stream of mercy, yet that mercy is living, and because living and personal, therefore fitting separately each part of our need; every character which comes before Him; all our trouble, all our sorrow. It possesses in itself both variety of character to meet every single heart, and movement of change, to pursue and accompany and save the sinner through all the stages of the course of salvation.

Take those three thoughts; the constant existence of our need; the constant persever- ance of the Saviour's love, hiding within itself the true moral, mental reality of the Passion, having in it now those elements of love which were expressed then in the precious blood- shedding; lastly, the various richness within that love to meet all the diverse poverty of

souls, the moving quickness with which it
follows all the changing perils of a single
spirit, all the cravings of renewed sonship,
all the steps of our restoration. These are the
great realities. And the Holy Spirit, "Who
proceedeth from the Father and the Son," and
also issues forth through the humanity of
Jesus Christ unto us, yet residing in Him in
fulness of Grace and Truth, He is at home in
our hearts, He knows His way to our thoughts,
to our needs. He can lift up this faculty of
ours which is our misery, our sinfulness, our
guilt, our emptiness; He can lift it up so as
to be not only capable but also filled with
the refreshment of the Divine Life out of the
Heart of Jesus Christ. He belongs to God
and man in Christ, and He knows His way to
each man's need. And if we pray to Him He
will bring us into the presence of the Saviour,
to be truly washed by the reality of His
Blood, to be truly brought home to God, truly
united one to the other in Christ, Who through
His Cross has made peace, bringing back those
who were alienated into the Home of God—
making them one by His blood.

Then further and just once more, as we
thus lie before God in our silent prayer, lifting
up our hearts in our hands unto Him, begging
for the Holy Spirit to bring us into the light
of Jesus Christ, the once crucified and now

ever living as a Lamb fresh slain upon the Altar
that is in the midst of the Throne of power
and love—as we thus pray to the Holy Ghost
we have one more great help from God; we
have the word of Jesus. This word comes to
be the completion of our desire; it comes to be
the spark for our love, to kindle us into true
sacrifice. It comes to be the very weapon
with which the Spirit will work, will pierce
our hearts, will loose our bonds, will set free
our feet. For this word of Jesus Christ is no
light unnecessary or failing word. The seven
words from the Cross are the words of " Him
who is real," [1] Who is the Truth, Who is
God; and they come forth by the necessity of
His Being, out of the fountain of His reality,
of His Love. They are the true expression,
the true explanation, the true revelation of
the real meaning and power of His Passion.
Finally, they are not only the words of Him
Who is true, words of revelation, telling us
what is waiting for us in Him; but they are
the words of Him Who is the Creator, they
are the words of Him Who is the Word
"through Whom all things were made"; and
therefore they not only reveal to us the secret
of His Heart, but they create in us by the
power of the Holy Ghost the answering power
to receive His Grace. They are the words of the

[1] 1 John v. 20.

true, and they are the words of the Creator,
which shall not return to Him empty, but
shall accomplish His saving will in us. By
these words there may be such a renewal in
consciousness and activity of the powers of the
regenerate life that we may be truly said even
to-day to be begotten again unto a lively hope
by the power of the Resurrection of Him
Whom now in the mystery of His Passion
we come to know through the help of the
Holy Ghost.

Let this be the direction of our devotion,
this the mode of our effort. We are come
to pray, we seek to know by the Holy
Ghost Jesus as He is in Heaven, yet we seek
to know Him according to the mystery of His
Passion, in those elements of His Heart which
were expressed in His blood-shedding. We
come to know Him, living, energizing, moving,
setting Himself side by side with each sinner
according to his character; moving along with
each man according to the progress of his
redemption. And we come to know Him
through His Holy words, adoring them as his
own utterance, recognizing in them the guide
to truth, determined not to put our meaning
into them but to seek that they may come, a
seed of truth, into our hearts. We come to
listen to the words of Him Who is the Truth,
and we come with hope because we come to

listen to the words of Him Who is the Creator.
And we pray that these holy seven utterances
sinking down into hearts not unprepared, made
soft by the dew of His grace, may through the
fostering power of the Holy Ghost bring forth
fruit in us unto everlasting life. And this we
do for ourselves one by one; for the holy
Church at large; for all poor sinners; for the
heathen and those lying destitute outside the
Gospel. Lastly, our prayer is for dying men
and women and children, who, by their dying
on this day, seem to claim a special share in
the prayers of those who come to profit by the
death of our Lord and Saviour Jesus Christ.

THE FIRST WORD

FATHER, FORGIVE THEM; FOR THEY KNOW NOT WHAT THEY DO

"Then said Jesus, Father, forgive them; for they know not what they do."—ST. LUKE xxiii. 34.

I HAVE, you see, set our aim low. There are higher things than those of which I spoke. There are souls empowered by God's visitation to enter into so loving a sympathy with Jesus Christ that they are indeed, in such a contemplation as we seek for, made the partakers of His inward passion. But, seeing that numbers of us are gathered together, we seek for something which is within the reach of all and to which the road is open and ready and plain for every one. In each Word, therefore, or after each Word I shall try to gather my thoughts under these three heads :— first we are to learn from the Saviour what is the sinner's need ; then we seek to know what is the cure He bestows upon that need ; and, thirdly, we ask what is the price which the God-Man has paid that we may

have the cure. Our need; the cure; the price.
Under these three heads time after time I invite you to offer your hearts in prayer to God.

So then, taking Him for our guide, we
learn from the first word what is the sinner's
first need. We learn—and the old lesson
needs continually to be re-learned—from the
first word of the Saviour on the Cross, that
the sinner's first evil is his guilt. There is the
first evil, there is the beginning of that which
has to be conquered piece by piece. The
sinner is at enmity with God. He is under
God's wrath, or his heart is filled with wrath
which is really and truly directed against God
Himself, his Father. And the cure for his
guilt—the cure for this first beginning of his
evil, the first thing which must be removed,
the first stone to be rolled away—the cure for
all this is free pardon, pure remission of sins.
There is a truth most familiar, and yet not
always operative. We forget that we must
have pardon to start with. We think of
pardon, of freedom from guilt, of peace with
God, as if it were the far-off end of a religious
life, as if it were the goal of many endeavours
which we might hope to attain to at the end
of a long life; and so we have to learn afresh
evermore that the beginning, the foundation,
the wicket-gate is peace, is remission, is
pardon. This is not the end of a Christian's

life, but this is its necessary beginning. There is no stirring in spiritual life whatsoever until we are in peace with God, and so this, which is the continual and abiding foundation of our life,—for all through " Mercy embraceth us on every side," and we must ever live as sinners continually forgiven—must be thought of also as the beginning. We forget this partly because we put off our repentance and are unwilling to disclose our faults until we have a better record with which to introduce them, and partly because we do not know how willing God is, how willing is the Saviour to pardon. We have to be reminded that long ago, before we even began to repent, yea even before we sinned, before we were born, "Christ died for the ungodly." Before there was a penitent on the earth, when all men were in rebellion, while we—mankind—were yet sinners, Christ died for the ungodly. And so as He mounts His Cross, when first He takes His place upon the Throne of intercession, He pleads first of all for pardon, to teach us for evermore that this is our first need, that we cannot even approach to the glory of His Cross excepting by the power of His prayer, and to teach us also that He is willing to save to the uttermost all those who come to God the Father by Him. You, my dear brethren, who have much to work out in your lives,

much which entangles, much which frets,
learn this, that the beginning of each day's
work of grace is receiving gently, patiently,
contentedly, the pardon which Jesus Christ
perpetually pleads for us, wins for us from the
Father. Enter in with a full assurance of
faith. We are justified from sin by the Blood
of Jesus Christ, and if we will but believe it
there is no longer any condemnation for those
who will come unto Christ Jesus and receive
the perfect remission of their sins—their oldest
sins, their newest sins, the sins of this morning, the sins from which we come to our
prayer, the sin which besets us in our
moments of silence—all this is perpetually
washed and cleansed by the Blood of Jesus
Christ. For this He prays for us still to-day
as He prayed in the first instant of His Crucifixion. "Father forgive them for they know
not what they do." Let us take that deeply
and practically to our hearts.

You also, dear brethren, who have entered
upon the life of prayer, who desire to know
Jesus and the Resurrection, who come day by
day to the work of meditation and find yourselves hindered and disappointed, ask yourselves whether what you need is not something surer to come by than any marvellous
or special visitation. What you need is only
this peace, pardon, the rolling away of guilt.

When this veil goes you shall see the Father in His mercy, the Face of the King, and shall be brought in by the Grace of Jesus Christ our Lord. And so, as we think of Him in our silence, nailed upon the cruel Cross, His Hands and His Feet pierced for our sins, and then the wood lifted up, and set with a cruel shock into the grave prepared for its foot, and the Saviour knowing and feeling the weight of the sins of the whole world in His flesh— for "He bare our sins in His own Body on the tree"—when you seek, in those thoughts which all through this time I do not attempt to express but leave to the love of your silent prayers, to apprehend Him in your silence, pray to Jesus Christ that He may not be disappointed of that which is His first object—our washing, our cleansing, our peace ; that initial beginning of the spiritual life which is the laying down of the arms which resist God, the ceasing to cry out against Him, the ceasing to cloak our sins, the setting up of our cross, which so opens the door of the heart that the pardon which is our Saviour's first will, penetrates and lays hold of all the being. Pray that this may be His, that He may not be disappointed of this.

Quærens me sedisti lassus,
Redemisti, crucem passus ;
Tantus labor non sit cassus.

Hang not in vain upon the cross for me! Pour not out in vain the love of pardon while my heart is closed, but grant with Thy gift of pardon also the gift of honesty, of the open heart, that the sins which have grown old in my conscience may to-day be washed away, that the sin which so easily besets me in spite of many repentances may to-day be caught and seized and destroyed by the power of thy love. Let the pardon of our Lord Jesus Christ, Who by the grace of God tasted death for all men, come unto me that He may have this for the beginning of His reward. And then before we part with this Word, think for a moment of the state of those for whom first He prayed, of their ignorance, for this is a consolation and an encouragement also for us. He prayed for them because of their ignorance —"They know not." Had they known what they were doing, says the Apostle, "They would not have crucified the Lord of Glory." They were deceived by the evil one, they were made his tools, they executed this un-speakable crime of slaying God in the Flesh, not knowing it. Therefore He prayed for their pardon. But remember, their ignorance was not a reason for their going without pardon. Their ignorance did not dispense them from their guilt, but their ignorance was His reason for making that prayer on their behalf, which because of their ignorance they could not make themselves. Put the ignorance, not next to the word "forgive"—"Father forgive them because they are ignorant," but take their ignorance to be the reason of the Saviour's prayer—"Father forgive them—I thy Son express their need for them because they know not what they do." Their ignorance does not dispense them from the need of pardon, but becomes in God's mercy their title to inherit the Saviour's prayer. For consider; their ignorance would not have led them into this great crime had they done the thing they knew; had each man done his duty in his place; had the false witness kept the law of Moses which he knew from his youth, "Thou shalt not bear false witness against thy neighbour"; had the people obeyed the sayings of the Psalms, which declare that the wicked slay the righteous man with the sword of their mouth, with the cry of their tongue; had the High Priests really ministered the Law; had Pilate done the duty of a faithful magistrate, there would have been no crime. For the avoidance of this unspeakable wrong there needed only that each man should do the duty which he knew, that each man should avoid the crime whose features were perfectly well known to him. They knew not that they crucified the Lord of

Glory, but they were not guiltless; because they were doing the characteristic actions of their life—the characteristic action of fallen man; they were persecuting the poor, they were slandering the brother, they were selfish, they were willing that one man should die for the people, they were unwilling to hear instruction, they would not pause to know, to repent, to let the light come into their hearts. And so their ignorance does not absolve them, they need for their absolution the blood of the Sinless Sufferer—the prayer of Jesus Who prays for them because they are ignorant, Who prays for us in our ignorance, Who sees our faults as we cannot see them, Who sees the iniquity even of our holy things, Who sees how dreadfully we have misused our life —our very bodily life sometimes. Fortune, opportunity, means of grace have been wasted. He knows all this as we do not, and we must cry to Him, " Saviour, plead for me not according to the guilt that I know, but according to the guilt that Thou alone knowest; pour down streams of cleansing, not according to my idea and knowledge of my need, but according to Thy sight of my blackness. And as before Thy sight I lie foul as foulness is in the sight of God, so pour down the abundance of mercy, mercy upon mercy through the merit of Thy saving Blood, that I may come to be clean as God counts cleanness, washed and made pure, whiter than snow. Even as now I am blacker than I know, make me to be whiter than I hope. Grant me the grace to enter in, to acknowledge this first need and to adore that which is its price—for the price of this first answer to our first need is the Saviour's accursedness —the Saviour's being made a curse for us. In order that we might be pardoned He was made sin; in order that we might be blessed and sacred He was made accursed, hanging upon the accursed tree. By his accursedness —by his acceptance of this sign and aspect and figure of guilt—by His taking upon Him the place of the sinner, we, who are sinners, enter into the place of the righteous, are accepted into the Home of the Father, are clothed with the robe that belongs to the good Son, and are accepted into the peace which we forfeited. Let it not be in vain. Now on your knees think of these three things.

Think of your need, pray God to show you your guilt; think of how fully He supplies that need with His abundant pardon; think of the price He has paid. He was made sin for us upon the accursed tree. Think of His pain, of His rejection, of how they mocked Him, of how they cast Him out as unworthy to be amongst them. Pray God to give us grace to put away false shame, to take to us the acknowledgment of the sins which He acknowledged for us; that we, now making that confession which He made for us Who is sinless, may become the righteousness of God in Him, through His grace Who, as He first mounted the Cross, prayed for the pardon which we need to-day, and which to-day He will pour out upon every soul in this place who kneels before Him in faith.

THE SECOND WORD

TO-DAY SHALT THOU BE WITH ME IN PARADISE

" And one of the malefactors which were hanged railed
on Him, saying, If Thou be Christ save Thyself and us.
But the other answering rebuked Him saying, Dost
not thou fear God, seeing thou art in the same condemnation? And we indeed justly; for we receive the
due reward of our deeds: but this man hath done
nothing amiss. And he said unto Jesus, Lord, remember me when thou comest into Thy Kingdom. And
Jesus said unto him, Verily I say unto thee, To-day
shalt thou be with Me in Paradise."—ST. LUKE xxiii.
39–43.

SURELY that blessed event, which was the
last event while the light still shone upon the
Cross before the supernatural darkness fell,
surely that helps us to understand, almost
to enter into, the joy that is in the Cross,
the joy that was in the Cross. We have to
remember that all through His Passion
Christ was filled with joy. His loving Heart,
so long straightened for mankind, is now
leaping forth in the accomplishment of salvation. He is quickened indeed in the Spirit,
though He be put to death in the flesh; and

as He suffers for us, His quickened Spirit
bursts out into preaching, into holy prophecy,
into the winning of souls. And here, just
after His first prayer, when He has in His
holy words set forth the meaning and purpose
of His Passion—to save the ignorant sinner
from the sin which he is too darkened to
confess—when He has set forth thus the great
purpose of His Passion, there followed the
glory of success; the one success which can
enlighten the heart of man here on earth, the
glory of turning a sinner from the error of
his ways, of adding one to the Kingdom of
the Father's love. This apostolic joy, this
essential joy of all Christians, which lies in
the spreading of the Redeemer's peace, this
was our Lord's; it came to Him for His great
consolation here in the opening of His Passion.
And let us recognize in this, in the good
thief's cry to Him, and his faith—that marvellous faith, by which he saw the Saviour, saw
His glory in spite of His humiliation, such a
faith as we can never show, for we have not
known Him until after He has been shown
to be the Son of God with power—let us
recognize in this faith the perpetual hopeful-
ness which is in man. Truly there must
never be despair of the sinner, no, not even of
our own sins. Our sins follow us. They tell
us our past is in us, and we have over and

over again been called upon to remember this
rootedness of our own sins in ourselves as a
cause for grief and for fear. I would rather
think of it as a cause of perpetual hope. Just
because the past deeds are not planted out
there in the wild of the world, but the old
guilt is here in the heart, therefore it is still
within the reach of the Saviour, of the Holy
Ghost, of the Father, Who by still keeping
my love, still keeping words of prayer upon
my lips, teaches me to hope, teaches me that
this very truth—that the sins of the past
accompany me all along the way of life—this
very fact is the title of my penitence, the
reason for my hope. For if the river of my
life bears thus all the volume of past actions,
if it has upon its bosom the stain of past disgrace, if it hides within its current the effect
of past foolishness; therefore that weakened
current, that stained surface, that volume of
faults, is here to-day passing through the
lock-gates, as it were, of a moment's experience, and may to-day be taken and arrested,
and turned by God, Who "turneth the hearts
of men as the rivers of water."

Years ago, a little boy, in a lesson about
sin, was taught that in sin it is as when
a child flies his kite carelessly and leaves
it fixed in some tree which he cannot
climb. There is the child below desiring to

undo his fault, but the symbol and the consequence of his mistake is up there aloft, tangled in the branches which he cannot touch. There is the hole through the window where the stone went, far above out of reach. Thus, we were taught, you can from your low station fling the missile which hurts, which kills, but you cannot climb up to cure, to save, to repair. Your sins must find you out. They lie there in the inaccessible past, in the distance of land and sea which you cannot cover, in the hearts of men which you cannot heal; and there is truth in all this. There are the consequences of our faults in others— alas! for that. But every one of those hearts in which the sin is, though it increases our fault, is the heart of one in the hands of the Father, in the hands of one wiser than we are. Our cure and the cure of others is not reserved for us. They lie near to God, and our guilt lies not there in the past. It has not clung to the darkened cloisters where we spent our school-days. Our foolish words do not linger there as a poisonous mist in the chambers where of old we played and worked, and were foolish and careless and idle. But they lie—the severe preacher tells it us—in our hearts, in our character, in our body, in the fibre of that movement which makes our daily life. There is the sole reality, there is the eternal consequence; and that, thank God, lies near beneath His hand. Life is like some river which, coming down from distant springs, yet still lies under the arch of sky, can still be moved, can still be turned, even as one of our great commanders in India once turned the current and direction of an immemorial stream, made it choose the alternative watershed, turned it from one side of a range of mountains, and made it water a province which, from past the memory of man, had been waterless. Even so God still presides at the fountain springs of our life. He is above our sin and shame. He is nearer even than our latest crime. He knows the way to us better than Satan does, who so tricks and plays upon us, making discord of the music of our lives. Nearer than sin, deeper than our shame and fear, closer than our closest grief, more our own than hands and frame, lies the Saviour's love, lies the Father's Heart, lies the power of the Spirit. There is always hope for us. He will take us, and turn us, and change us. Yea to-day, if we bring this stream, in the division of it which we call to-day—that is enough for Him—to His feet, He will so change and cleanse it that it shall be pure, yea even to its springs. That is what the lesson of the thief teaches us—the perpetual possibility of reform.

But then we must go on to ask from our
Saviour what is the second need that He sees in
us, what is the second cure, and what the price
paid down for it. After pardon, what then?
After guilt; is all well when guilt is done
away? No, there remains pain, suffering, death.
The poor thief was pardoned, was reconciled;
but he was not taken down from his cross.
The cruel pain still clutched him, creeping
closer and closer to the seat of life, the deadly
weight of his sin-stained body still wrenched
him on the tree. He had to bear all the evil,
he had to go further even than the Saviour
of the world, he had to bear that last strain
which God refused to let Jesus inherit, because a bone of him might not be broken.
But the thief's limbs were broken by the cruel
bar of the spear. He had to go through all
the long agony, the interminable history as it
must have seemed, of a slow dying, after his
pardon. And so, after guilt is shaken off,
after God becomes our friend, after justice has
no terrors for us—because we are in Christ
Jesus, walking not according to the flesh
but according to the spirit—there remains
the passion, there remains the Cross, the
sorrow, the trial, the long, long pain. And
what does Jesus give us for its cure, for its
support, to enable us to sustain it? What
is His cup of water to maintain the re-

conciled sinner through his long crucifixion
of the flesh? He gives us the true cure,
the grace of patience; and for the source of
patience He gives us hope. Remember that.
Patience is the cure for pain; not escape,
but the power to bear. And the medicine
for anguish, the food of patience is always
hope; not mere manly cries, not the shout
of encouragement of the military chief like
Frederick the Great, who calls upon his men
to charge, scorning and mocking them as they
hang back, asking them if they mean to live
for ever; not the mere brusquerie of comrade-
ship, but the sweet medicine of reward, of
hope. The promise, that is the Saviour's
pledge to build up patience, that is His way
of ministering to pain. He gives us the
promise as to the penitent thief, of the Paradise that we need. Cast it not away from
you, that promise. Think not in your modern
manliness to do without the old stories of the
heavenly reward, of the golden city, of the
rest in Paradise with Jesus. Think not that
we can be more courageous than the Saviour,
more manly than God's rule, but understand
that He has given us the thought and memory
of Heaven to be the standing bulwark of
patience, to enable us day by day, hour by
hour, to endure that which He would have us
to endure. And consider how much wiser we

should be if we still loved to think about,
to rejoice, as they scorn us for rejoicing, in
this thought of Heaven, rather than to find
the medicine of our grief in worldly distrac-
tion; in the invention of fleshly delight, in
the selfishness of earthly money-getting and
money-spending upon ourselves. How much
better to bear the Cross, enduring the shame,
as Jesus was not too great to bear it; because
of the hope set before Him, He endured the
Cross, despising the shame. By the prospect
of Paradise, by the promise of the garden, by
the word of sweet companionship with Himself in secure rest, He made the poor thief able
to bear his torture, his grief, his death. He
held him up by promises, by hope, by tender
sympathy, so teaching us how we must en-
courage one another, how we, as we look
upon the poor, and upon the suffering, must
build them up through hope, through promise,
by speaking of the heavenly place, by
leading them to where Jesus Christ already
wipes away all tears from our eyes. He
teaches us to accept this as the means of our
own endurance, that we, not thinking any
of God's gifts unnecessary, taking that which
He offers, may do that which He expects, may
bear the pain which He puts upon us, now
that we are pardoned, not before; because
while we are in guilt we cannot bear the Cross,

but when we are pardoned He bestows upon us the community of His sufferings.

In your thoughts just now upon your knees pray for all poor men who are reaping the earthly consequences of their faults. Some of you perhaps belong to a Society which we know of, in which we pray for the poor men who are about to suffer the penalty of death for crimes against life. Pray for such as those to-day. Beg for them a complete pardon. Remember what we said of hope accompanying the sinner all along his life. Just because the sinner is himself, just because the book of God is here in the breast, therefore God can wipe out the evil record. Pray for them; let that be your first thought. And then, secondly, accept from Jesus His privilege of pain. Say to Him, "Now that I am pardoned, now I have peace, put upon me the Cross, give me my share of the world's great pain; let me know the suffering of the poor, of the weary, of the solitary. Let me take my own share bravely." Thirdly, acknowledge, recognize, accept, that which is Christ's cure for grief, that which is Christ's food for patience, the food of hope, the prospect of the heavenly home. Say to Him now, "Jesus, remember me when Thou comest into Thy Kingdom." Say to Him, those of you who are in grief, those of you who have sickness,

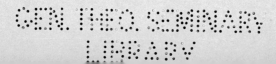

who have anxiety, who have solitude, who are old, who are alone; say to Him, "Lord, we suffer; but we indeed justly, for we receive only the due reward of our deeds; but Thou Who hast done nothing amiss, remember us when Thou comest into Thy Kingdom," and He will give you to-day the promise and almost its fulfilment; you shall be already "saved in hope." He will give you to walk with Him to-day in peace in the Paradise which He has opened for you through His Blood.

THE THIRD WORD

BEHOLD THY SON! BEHOLD THY MOTHER

" When Jesus therefore saw His mother, and the disciple standing by, whom He loved, He saith unto His mother, Woman, behold thy son! Then saith He to the disciple, Behold thy mother."—ST. JOHN xix. 26, 27.

LIFT your hearts once again, my brethren, to Jesus Christ in Heaven, and say to Him "Lord, show us, show me, what is my next need; what is the next evil Thou wouldest cure in me as I come forward in the life of salvation." And He makes answer thus: "Look, my Son, to My Cross; hear what I said and did there; I teach thee in Myself what is thy need, paying for thee piece by piece all the price of thy salvation." And so we read, "There stood by the Cross of Jesus, His mother and His mother's sister, Mary the wife of Cleophas and Mary Magdalene. When Jesus therefore saw His mother, and the disciple standing by whom He loved, He saith unto His mother, Woman, behold thy son. Then saith He to the disciple, Behold thy mother. And from that hour that disciple took her unto his own home."

There the Lord teaches us what is the third part of our need ; what the evil is, what the cure and what the price. What does the sinner need when he has made the first step of penitence, when he has confessed his sin, when he has set himself to turn away from evil habits, when he is bearing manfully his penance, when he knows what it is to work out the painful consequences of a wasted life— what does he want then ? Do you know—or have you never known it because you have never lacked that precious thing—a home ? That is what the sinner needs, that is what the penitent cries out for. This we know who have lived as clergymen in the thickly-popu-lated parts of our City, who have seen dear fellows come out from the herded life of the great lodging-houses, where there are good men and bad as in other places, but which are in themselves a kind of symbol of a wretched lonely life in a crowd. We know what they want. In my old home down in Southwark there were night after night some-thing like a thousand single men sleeping within a stone's throw from my own bed— eight hundred men on the left-hand side, nearly a hundred across the road, fifty or sixty down below my window in the next houses to our own. We know what that lonely life is—of the wandering man who has no wife or children or who has lost them by his fault or theirs. And we know what happens when such a one—I am not speaking as if all were bad or were more bad than any other class of men—we know what the cry is when one of these comes to church, confesses his sins, shows his wounds, gets absolution, begins to be regular in his attendance, longs to be good, bears his suffering. For indeed he has much to bear, a bad character to fight against, scoffs from those who knew him of old, frowns from the respectable tradesmen who will not risk to engage him. All this he bears, perhaps in bodily sickness, on scanty food, and in pain. When he has made his first two stages, when he has shown his conscience, when he has shouldered his cross, what is his next cry? What does he say to his clergyman?—he says "Father, you must get me a home—I must have some place which shall be more or less my own. I cannot go on living in this barrack way with no ground for myself beyond the limit of my bed, where I cannot so much as leave my coat during the day, but must carry everything about with me wherever I go. There must be a home. Give me a sense of belonging to somebody. Get me"—this is the word in nine cases out of ten—"get

me into a family.   Persuade one of the people,
one of the married folk, to make me a lodger.
Let me have a door to knock at when I come
home late ; let there be a voice to scold me
when I come back wrong." He wants above
all other things a home—a reconstruction of
the old feeling, the old atmosphere. If he
could but get back his mother, his father, his
wife, who perhaps has barred the door against
him. That is his need—a home. And that
quite strictly and always and according to
the essential order of spiritual need, is what
every one of us wants as we advance in the
life of restoration. Jesus knew this, as He
knew all things. He read our hearts there
from the Cross. He knew that for ever to the
end of time this would be the sinner's, the
penitent's need. And so He bestowed upon
us in the third place the cure of solitude ; and
He paid the price, He paid down the price of
His mother's companionship. He elected to
die alone, untended, without one eye to watch
his latest breath. He chose to die without
one face upon which His gaze might rest, in
order thus to pay down the price for the essential need of every sinner, to give to every
sinner a home, a brother, a mother. See how
piece by piece He pays down the very price.
It is, as we said during the week, not only a
ransom—a sum of money paid for the con-

demned—but life for life, soul for soul, His peace given for our peace, His honour given for our restoration, His pain paid down that we might have hope. That He might save others He refused to save Himself. He shuts off the hope of coming down from the Cross that He may with authority speak to the thief of the Paradise to come. And so, that He may with authority give us the home we need, He pays down the price of His own home, He gives His own mother, the unspeakably dear, unspeakably worthy of affection. The mother who is incomparable—for her Son need not, cannot come into any comparison—she who stands up above the sons of men, the chosen maiden of the Lord, the mother of Our Lord and God Jesus Christ, the shrine of Godhead, the fountain enclosed, the garden of God's election—she is given up by Him who loved her unspeakably, Whom she with the perfect fulfilment of a creature's love cherished and held in a mother's heart. Through her heart also must go the sword. Think it not a phrase, or a fancy. She was a real mother with a real mother's love. You who are mothers yourselves, think how it is with you when the strong son comes back from over seas to die; when you find him again in his narrow lodging or in the hospital bed, and see his great muscular frame shaken through the disease of his

chest; and by the rasping breathing know
that he is passing from you, and know that he
knows. Think of it you who are in the way
to see this sight—the clergyman, the doctor,
the friend—who see the little woman by the
bedside, and it seems hardly credible that she
nursed on her breast the giant who draws his
labouring breath. Think of that pain, that
cross, that sword through the heart. And
then think of Mary the mother of the Lord,
and how He turned from her, how He relin-
quished her, how He bade her go home, how
He parted with her comfort. He was lifted
up above her; she could not reach that hard
bed upon which He lay, she could not minister
to His thirst, she had no reed to lift the
sponge upon. But He parted even with the
sight of the eyes which overflowed with love
of Him; He gave away His Home that He
might be wholly poor, and that by paying
down this price—this price of domestic love,
this treasure of a mother's companionship—He
might win for ever for all sinners that which
they essentially need, the companionship,
the home, the love of a mother. So He
gave away His mother, He gave away His
beloved disciple. He gave them to each
other, thus creating a home even as He sacri-
ficed His home, and re-creating our homes
by His homelessness upon the Cross. That

is our third grief, that is our third wound; homelessness, solitude. That is His third cure; a home for all, a family. He is God "Who setteth the solitary in families, Who maketh men to be of one mind in a house," "Who maketh Himself households like a flock of sheep," devising "means that His banished be not expelled from Him."

We may not to-day dwell upon all this, lest we encroach upon your time of prayer. Think of the home which He has given you, in the order of nature. Think how precious it is; think how it is the very thing you need. Think how Jesus loved it—loves it now. Think how He restores you that love which in the course of nature passes away. He has loved us in our families; He loves our fathers, our mothers. And as a true friend makes a kind of exchange and would have us know his mother as he knows ours, so Jesus, the Friend of sinners, invites us to love Mary. He says, "I have loved your mothers that bore you. Do not you care for Mine who bore Me?" We must love His mother as He has so well loved ours. And she becomes in a way our own also, for we are in Him. He is ours and we are His, and with Him we take this love of His dear mother, whose pain He endured to see upon the Cross, whose turning away in so much grief was perhaps the sharpest grief to

Him. He invites us to this love. And to all those who in the course of nature or in other ways have passed away from home life, he offers the supernatural home; to all He offers the great house of God the Father—the Church which is God's habitation. There we are all to be at home. Think not then of this word Church as being a hard word of discipline—of organization. Think of the Church as being the home of love—the loving congregation of brothers round the feet of the Father through the merit of Jesus, breathed upon like some garden of flowers by the gale of the Holy Ghost. Ah! that is a great thing that we need. That is a great gain for us when we come to see the Church as it is, when we know and understand that no hard uniformity, no historical pride satisfies the true account, the true meaning of the Church; when it comes to be to us a garden of flowers where a fountain is in the midst, even Jesus—"the fountain of gardens, the well of living waters and streams from Lebanon"; when it comes to be the Father's Home, and every one in it is a dear brother, and every woman in it is sacred for Mary's sake—for Jesus' sake; when we cease to strive one against another, when we pray God to forgive us for our selfishness, when we seek to bestow ourselves one upon the other in brotherly love.

And even on such a day as this I cannot refrain from saying one further word for peace. As we come for the peace that we need, as we come round that Table, which is the Supper Table of our heavenly home, as we come to eat the Bread of Life, Jesus Christ, see that there is pity, see that there is compassion, considerateness, "tarrying one for the other." Here is the true ritual of the Altar. No recovery of ancient symbols, of Catholic ceremonial, will make the Sanctuary anything but poor and bare and mean while there is one soul hindered, one soul offended, one man needlessly kept away from the Table of the Lord. Think of that. That is what the Lord desires to see—His Holy Table surrounded by sympathy, courtesy, gentleness, brotherly love, mutual compassion, the cloud of the incense of happy prayer. That is what He requires— the ceremonial of an unfailing courtesy, the richness of a family drawn together round His feet; the true antiquity, the true catholic dignity, of the poor coming where the poor man's friend waits for them. Let us not be content while this holy mystery has around it anything which offends, anything which checks, anything which perplexes. And since there is no other conceivable means by which everybody may be happy, everybody contented, everybody find the form and frame of

worship which suits his soul, therefore let
there be diversity. Remember this when you
emerge from the warm feelings, from the
hearty prayers of Holy Week. Do not return
to the old fight for a mechanical regularity,
for a heartless uniformity; but remember that
what Jesus desires to see is contented hearts
round about Him. Let those, therefore, who
can love and use the ancient Catholic ceremonial of the Church, be content—as I think
they are fully content—that others should
still retain the barer worship of our childhood;
and let those on the other hand who are
offended and checked by things which are
practically new although they are historically
ancient, let them not grudge a different way to
those who are differently moved. And let us
all believe that peace is what we want; not
uniformity in outward things, but the true
harmony of contented hearts; that since one
church and one altar cannot possibly in the
nature of things present exactly the aspect
which all Christians would like to see, but
every form must needs offend in some sense
some; therefore in the great mansion of God's
Church let there be many chambers of approach to the one Bread, that in the midst of
a certain diversity of mode we may draw
together without check, without alarm, without shame, without debate, with mutual

courtesy, tarrying one for the other, in unbroken pity, to Jesus Christ Who is our Peace. Think not that this is too low a thing to have spoken of to-day. Keep it in your prayers. You will be called upon to return presently to the old debates. Refuse them. By the Passion of Jesus, by the mercies of God—I speak to you in God's Name, and you shall hardly be guiltless if you refuse to hear—if there be any consolation in Christ, any love of the Spirit, I call upon you to avoid all those debates which bring the indignity of discord within sight, within hearing, within thought of the sacred mystery of God's home and the spread table of God's family, into which may He grant to us sinners full entrance for our souls' salvation.

In your silence pray God that you may know your homelessness; pray God to grant you the incoming to His home; pray God to make you, with Mary and all Saints, loyal fellow-brothers and sisters in the great family of Grace.

THE FOURTH WORD

ELI, ELI, LAMA SABACHTHANI?

"And about the ninth hour Jesus cried with a loud voice, saying, Eli, Eli, lama sabachthani? that is to say, My God, My God, why hast Thou forsaken Me?"—St. Matt. xxvii. 46.

This is the moment, dear brothers, in the great lesson from the Cross at which we have specially to beg the grace of a renewed resolution of attention. Let us be swift to hear, to receive the engrafted word which is able to save our souls. Even as you have persevered so patiently in your action of devotion in this sacred place, so maintain and renew with ever fresh courage your desire to ascend to Christ in Heaven, to learn from Him the secret of His sorrow and His peace. Ask of Him yet once again, "What do I need now, O Christ?" Learn the need by this wonder of the word in the darkness. There fell a supernatural darkness over the land from the sixth to the ninth hour; and about the ninth hour, towards the end of His Passion, almost at the very end,

Jesus cried with a loud voice, saying, " Eloi, Eloi, Lama sabachthani ? " that is, " My God, My God, why hast Thou forsaken me ?"—crying out in a voice which those who heard it did not understand because they were not used to the sacred language of the scriptures; crying out in a voice which we still cannot and dare not understand ; expressing some of the mystery of a holy desolation in His creaturely nature, bearing witness to a darkness which was due not to Him, but to us—the darkness of the separation from the sight of God's Face which He knew while He dwelt unchanged in the light which no man can approach unto. For in that light He was all through His Passion, yet nevertheless the darkness fell upon the soul of Jesus Christ according to the mystery of His sacred humanity. That voice, whose meaning regarding Him we hardly dare to search after, may well be studied by our low method. For we can ask with regard to it with a good courage and with perfect security : What is its message for the sinner's need ; what does it tell us of the evil that is in us; what is the feature of our poverty which God will next cure—what is the cure and what is the price that is paid for the cure ?

The sinner begins with penitence, and he must make every part of his journey with penitence unto the end of the way. The need

of penitence comes first, not in such sense as to
pass away as if its work were done, but so as
to be the continual foundation upon which
every day of spiritual life must be built up.
Penitence never passes away. The Church we
are brought into is a body of mercy—" Mercy
embraceth us on every side." We are there
among the redeemed, among the forgiven,
always as men ransomed ; and in Heaven those
who stand clothed in the white raiment of an
accomplished righteousness, bear witness that
they washed their robes from stains in the
Blood of Jesus ; and the song they sing is the
song of Moses and of the Lamb, the song of the
Red Sea and of the Precious Blood, the song
of deliverance from slavery, of redemption
from sin and condemnation. Nay, the very
object of their worship is revealed in such wise
as ever to maintain the sense of mercy and of
a sacrifice. He stands as if a lamb late slain
upon the altar in the midst of the Throne, He
that liveth and was dead ; and the secure joy
with which they adore Him is a joy of penitence transfigured into praise. So the first
necessity, and the constant necessity of the
life of grace is penitence. And the second is
akin to it ; it is a constant hope in constant
patience, a glad submission under pain until
the Kingdom comes ; and then thirdly, is the
need and gift of Home. And can there be

anything wanted more than this—anything to
be coveted by those who are brought into the
Home and are no more strangers and pilgrims,
but fellow-citizens with the Saints and belong
to the household, the family of God?

Yes, there is something more. There is
such a thing as being in the Palace and not
knowing the King. There is such a thing as
being safe in a certain sense in the family and
not knowing the Father by face; knowing
Him perhaps by name, remembering Him
sometimes, but not dwelling in the light of
His countenance. And so I said well, now is
the time to persevere, for this is the evil, not
of the world, but of the Church. This is the
sadness not of the reprobate, but of the penitent. This is the penury not of the unbeliever,
but of the Catholic. He is in the Church, he
enjoys the sacraments, but he has not sought
to press through beyond the veil. He receives
the precious gifts of God as if in costly caskets,
but he has not broken the vase that the frag-
rance might fill the whole house. He dwells
under the protection of the Saviour's name,
but he cannot tell from his experience that
Christ is in him of a truth. And yet he is
not reprobate. The words have a meaning,
though they have no thrill for him, which say
"We are come unto Mount Sion." He lives
with his face averted. His heart is locked up

from prayer. At the best there are words, there are memories of Christ, of God the Father; at best there is a belief in the Holy Ghost as a kind of third consequence in the Creed, which we believe in because we believe in the Father and the Son; as a Somewhat on the far outward confines of our territory of faith instead of a Presence which is the continual inward treasure of our conscious- ness, the earnest of our inheritance, the prize in hand, the light we know already, the *witness* to the things as yet unseen. God's presence, God's love, God's face, the power of the Holy Ghost, the aspect of Jesus, the fellowship of the Father's love—these were not meant to be subjects for our conjecture; they were meant to be the grounds of our conviction, to be that which we allege in sup- port of faith and hope, not that which we faintly endeavour to infer as the result of a logi- cal speculation. What is the meaning of the weakness of Christian evidences? What is the meaning of Christians being shaken in faith? Do you not know Him, the Father? "Ye have an unction of the Holy One and ye know all things." "Do ye not recognize about yourselves," asks St. Paul, "is not this the fruit of your daily self-inspection, that Christ is in you of a truth, except ye be reprobate?" "Christ in you, the hope of glory," is He unvisited? Does He live within your heart unknown? Your Father in Heaven—can you not go into His Presence? Do you not know what it is to lie speechless before Him in prayer, so near to Him that there can be no address, because your heart is in His Heart, even as the beloved disciple laid his head upon the breast of God Incarnate? We are not only to be in the privileged body, inheritors of the Kingdom, having the *entrée* to the Court, but we are to be of those who know the Father, the King, the Eternal, the unspeakable beauty, who are filled as with new wine with the joy of His Presence. We should not fear criticism then, we should not fear unbelief; our persuasion, our apologetic would not take the form it sometimes takes, of an almost despairing effort to find some other man to keep us in countenance while we are Christians; to win some one, great or small, to bear us out in the faith of Jesus Christ. No, we should know Him and the power of His resurrection, if we were made conformable to His death. That is the need. If you know it not, if it does not sound to you like a need, does that mean that you have it like the home? No, it means that you do not know how near God can be, how familiar the Father is, how God, as Dame Julian of Norwich says, " Willeth to be known; " it means, you do not know what is

the glory of the liberty of the children of God,
and what the protecting tenderness of their
Father, the Father of our Lord Jesus, Who in
Him blesses them with all spiritual blessings
in the heavenly places. And indeed it is far
far better for us to feel desolate, to feel solitary,
to feel in the dark. If we are not conscious
of God's Presence, it is good at least to be
conscious of His absence, though in fact He is
not far from any one of us. And all those who
know Him well, so greatly desire to know Him
better that they are ready to cry out, " My
God, my God, why hast Thou forsaken me?"
It was because of His nearness that Jesus so
cried; it was because of His knowledge, that
the darkness was a darkness to His illuminated
eye; and if we are in Him and living by
Him we shall not think we have attained;
but just because we are being pressed closer
and closer to the Father's heart, we shall cry
out, "How long, O Lord—how long before
Thy love comes home, how long before the
heart is yielded, how long before I know and
see?" "We should better find God," says
one of the old Puritans,[1] " we should sooner
find God to be our Father if we were more
orphaned in our spirit—He is the Father of
the fatherless, and the God of the widow,

[1] Sibbes (in effect). The words which follow are not a
quotation.

and it is the soul that knows its widowhood
that finds the husbandhood of God ; it is the
heart that feels fatherless which has Him for a
Father." That is what the sinner needs—he
cannot be safe without that. This is no privilege of rapture for one Saint in a thousand ;
this is no marvel for a Saint Teresa ; for a
Saint John of the Cross. It is the essence of
the forgiven life ; it is the necessary consequence of a true penitence ; it is what we must
all press on to, to know Him Whom we have
believed in, seeking after Jesus Christ beyond
the sky, and in Him finding the fulness of the
Father's glory. To follow on to know the
Lord—that is the prize He bestows upon the
sinner. First pardon, and then patience ; and
then a home so rich, full of all the supplies of
grace ; and then there breathes through the
corridors of the house an inviting voice, and
those who know declare the voice of the
Father Who comes home although he never
departs ; Who makes Himself heard although
He was never silent ; Who invites although
He has led us by the hand ; Who would have
us listen, lend our ears, come to Him. Be
silent, yield the heart, that here in this life
we may know Him the only true God and
Jesus Christ whom He has sent. It was to
gain this that Christ died ; not that we might
be superficially washed only ; not that we might
be pardoned and then left alone ; not that we

might be gathered together and kept safe as in a caravan, as in an ark; but that we might be drawn up into the Father's heart. This is perfection, this is goodness, this is pardon. If we stop short of this we are not cleansed. Even as cleansing means union—"Except I wash you ye have no part in me"—so union means pardon; unless we are in union, the pardon halts and is not certain. We are cleansed that we may pass the threshold; we pass the threshold that we may be clothed upon with the marriage garment; we have the marriage garment in order that we may go in to the wedding supper of the Lamb—a feast which is a feast of marriage, a feast of union; and the love of Jesus Christ is not satisfied with being the love of a King who pardons, of a Lord who pays the price, of a friend who risks, who lays down, his life; it is only satisfied when it becomes the love of the bridegroom for the bride, when it avails to compel union, to yield all His life for us, to win our life to God, Who so loves us that He gave, and yet gives, His only-begotten Son. The exaltation of the humble heart into the eternal bliss of God Who waits for us—that is what the sinner next needs; the joy of communion, of contemplation, of knowing Him Whom he hath believed, of tasting the sweetness of that Bread which he receives sacramentally at the Altar, of recognizing in his heart the cry of the Spirit of adoption, the adoption in which he was constituted by the life-giving sacrament of baptism. To know God Who has known us, "to press on that I may apprehend, seeing that also I was apprehended by Jesus Christ," this is our prize, this is our need, nothing less than this will save us. And see how great a price Jesus paid for it. He paid down the price of His own mysterious desolation. Even as to give us our home on earth, His Catholic Church, He paid down the price of His mother's tears, He watched the sword go through her own heart also; even so, to give us the joy of the Father's face He paid down in a mystery we cannot fathom the price of His own darkness, of His own desolation. He hung there solitary that we might come home. He made Himself a stranger and forsaken that we, who were strangers and alienated from the life of God, might be brought in and made partakers of that Eternal Rest from which Jesus Christ sprang forth towards us, in order that completing His glorious circuit of life He might sweep us on the stream of His answering love of God into that Heart of the Father, which is His home eternally, and which He makes to be ours. He has made us free of the Home, of the Heart, of the Face of God. " If the Son shall make you free, ye shall be free indeed "—made sons, partakers, entering into the knowledge of the Father. Ah! it is this holy knowledge we must long for, if the Saviour is to see in us the travail of His Soul.

Pray then to God now, in this hour, to give you the knowledge of your desolation; pray God to give you, it may be even now, those who have not yet known it, the wondrous entrance into His—I almost dare to say—unveiled presence. "Seek ye the Lord while He may be found, call ye upon Him while He is near." Pray to Him that you may never waste that price of your home-coming which was His desolation, but entering under the shadow of His prayer, "My God, My God," may have your solitude cured, to the glory of God the Father. And those who have known, those who have lost, or deem they have lost, that Presence—must they despair? Believe it, the darkness they walk in is the very road to the clearer light, for it is the way of the companionship of Jesus. "Who is among you that feareth the Lord, that obeyeth the voice of His Servant, that walketh in darkness and hath no light? Let him trust in the name of the Lord," Who is called Saviour; "let him stay upon his God," Who is Emmanuel, God with us, and Who not only heals us by His stripes, but, by the merits of His desolation, "receives us unto the Glory of God."

THE FIFTH WORD

I THIRST

"After this, Jesus knowing that all things were now accomplished, that the Scripture might be fulfilled, saith, I thirst."—ST. JOHN xix. 28.

WE must still keep on our low level, by our low method, asking yet once again what need in us the Saviour reveals by His word. Well indeed if by His grace we can know it and receive its cure. We shall then indeed be celebrating His Passion although after a low fashion, yet in a way fit for us and really bringing Him honour. What then does the sinner come to know within himself, if by God's mercy he does attain to some communion with God, some experience of those heavenly realities into which he is knit up by his membership in the Church? Can there be anything more for him? In one sense all is done, even as of our Lord it is said that He knew "that all things were now accomplished." The man has, in the centre of his life, reached the goal, which is God. But the great work is

125

being done on the stage of a creaturely life,
and in a world of change and time ; and goes
in advance of the perfect practical conquest of
the man's mind and flesh.   He enters by faith
into the glory of God, but there yet remains
the work of conforming all the being and all
the circumstances to God.   And so in your
experience you will recognize that there is
something which seems an anti-climax—a great
disappointment.   We come out of darkness
into light, we repent, we give ourselves to the
Church, we live as good Christians, as good
Catholics, we frequent the Sacraments ; and
then we are drawn on further to the life of
prayer, and that which had been to us only a
thought becomes a golden key to open up our
very hearts to the heavenly glory ; and we think
that now surely all is accomplished.   Now, cries
the forgiven soul, now let me die ; I shall be
no better.   But then God, having thus given
us the rudiments of Faith—for that heavenly
vision is only the normal state of a Christian
recovered after so long a lapse—now begins to
use us.   Having drilled His soldier He takes
him from the parade-ground ; He leads him
forth to battle ; He throws him again among
men.   There is a pause in the sweet flood of
sensible devotion ; the tears flow no longer ; the
man comes back again as it were to this lower
world ; he has to work out his salvation with

fear and trembling, and in the discipline of
ordinary experience. He has his place in the
organization of life, in the world, in the state ;
he returns, in a sense, from the heavenly vision,
not disobedient. Yet he goes back as Paul
went back, to the long roads, to the troublesome
people, to the wearisome apostolate, to the
journeys, so eventful and so undistinguished.
And the shipwrecks and the trials, and the
lodging in Rome—all the common incidents
of a prosaic discipline—come to him after he
has been lifted up, " Whether in the body or
out of the body I cannot tell," into the third
heaven, where he has heard unspeakable
words, and known something of " a crown laid
up." And in the converted man to-day it is
the same, in measure ; and he needs a warning
and an encouragement when he drops from his
rapture, from his prayer, from his delight,
from his unbroken rest, and finds himself again
hurried from point to point, attending in the
police-courts, paying his way, governing his
parish, working out his business. He has to
be assured that this lies all in the track. By
this as by some hammering God secures the
great gift. He warmed you to red-heat in the
fire of His love, and now He puts you on the
anvil of His providence, that by the blows of
His discipline He may shape you according to
the model of His expectations. Now you find

the hammering of a smithy, into which the irons are flung in crowds, for shaping and reshaping, and it is precisely this which is salvation, though it appears in an order so unexpected. It is here in the ordinary perplexities of life—the things to take, and the things to leave aside, the feasting and the fast, and the more difficult interior mortification of eating when other men can fast. It is the level common-sense life of health and weakness; of home, and care and anxiety; the prosaic life of the married clergyman who comes down from the vision of a strange and separate perfection, to find himself as other men; it is this which is the appointed discipline by which God beats home the precious pattern of His design upon the metal which He heated high in the flame of rapture and generous desire. And so in our Lord there was this after the climax of suffering. After the darkness and eclipse, after that pinnacle of pain which no man can search into, comes this common want—the common want of thirst. The discipline of the Cross in its acutest torture was designed by man; but this was only such a thing as accompanies all work, that which belongs to the Cross, not as a passion but as a labour—that which comes to all men in the course of the hours, but which comes in torrents of power in such pain as His. Yet it was a

common want, a common pain ; lifted up into
the extreme of urgency by the extremity of
His pain—but still a common want. And,
mark you, a want which He allows to be ministered unto, which He allows to be relieved.
When they brought to Him before His Passion
the mingled drink of wine and myrrh, which
was meant to soften His pain, which was, we
are sometimes told, ministered by some guild of
pious women to all condemned sufferers that
it might deaden the terrible torture of the
execution—when this came He rejected it. He
would have nothing unnecessary, nothing to
obscure the full agony of His pain. He would
taste death for every man by the grace of God
and by nothing else. He, by the grace of God,
lifted up by the power of God, would taste
death for every man. But now in this common
want, in this thirst which He shares with the
animals as they drag their loads, at last He allows
Himself to be ministered to. And He teaches
thereby that most penetrating kind of mortification, the inward mortification in which we
acknowledge our common needs and accept
their common remedy. He accepted the drink
because He was thirsty. He tasted of it,
according to the scriptures; but also according to the truth of His Humanity. Think
how beautiful it is that after all upon the Cross,
at last, He stooped low enough to find our pity

I

where it lay hid. We cared not for Him
because He was our God; we blasphemed Him
and smote Him on the mouth. He came in
His title of Prophet, and the cry was, "Thou
art a liar, and possessed of a devil." He came
with the proclamation, "Behold your King,"
and we cried, "Away with Him, away with
Him; we will not have this Man to rule over
us!" He came to us as our brother, our fellow-
creature; and we heaped upon Him indignity,
we smote Him, and spat upon Him, and
scourged Him, we put Him outside the pale of
our common humanity. But, when at last He
cries out, in a voice which might be the voice
of the beasts that perish, when He owns a want
which He shares with the poor creatures of
burden, man's pity is at last found out. There
low down it lurks. Even so now you may see
it. The men who care not for God, the men
who do not take pity upon Jesus Christ, the
men who ruin women's souls, the men who
neglect their own little children—see them in
a crowd in their drink, in their carelessness,
by the street side, when they have no thought
but of some pleasure, some bet or loud gaiety;
see them if a child stands in danger as
a van swings past the corner. From the
crowd of careless sinners, of rough and
reckless men and women, there will come the
cry of pity, of alarm; they spring to save;

they cannot bear that pain; they will save the
poor child's limbs. And though men seem like
hardened steel, yet the sight of suffering will
touch us all. The rough man is sorry for his
horse; he puts his horse out of misery; cannot
bear to see the poor thing wounded and in
despair. That is a great blessing to think of;
that there is a soft place left in our hearts.
God pursues us down and down, and although
we reject Him once and again, and build up
barriers round our feelings, yet He makes His
way in by the rudimentary appeal of common
pain, common woes that we still feel; there is
still a slender thread by which God may disentangle the dark maze of our wilfulness, and
find His way into our poor souls. Be glad,
then, that on the Cross, even He Who was
rejected of men, Who was led as a lamb to the
slaughter, found among His butchers pity;
found one to lift up the sponge moistened in
the sour wine left for the executioners' refreshment, dipped out of their common stock. They
did not grudge Him a drink of their wine when
He cried, "I thirst!" There was one ready, according to prophecy, to give Him that. There
then is that great blessing; and in this we see
the Lord's great condescension, that He is willing
to receive something so much less than our best.
If He cannot have our faith, our love, He will
accept our money, our generosity. From the

adulterer, from the robber, from the thief, from
the man of pleasure, He will still accept alms.
He is satisfied—no, He is not satisfied, but He
will not reject it as we should.   The clergyman,
however broad in mind, however full of love,
can hardly bear to take it; can hardly bear to
think that God's work is kept up, for example,
as I knew a good work kept up once, by the
alms of a betting man.   We can hardly bear
to take such help, but Jesus will take it.   If
you are not sorry for yourselves He is glad
you are sorry for your children.   If you will
not cease from selling the poison which brings
men to death, He will accept—and He will
use—the alms with which you try to make up
feebly for the wrong you do.   He does not
reject it as we should be tempted to reject it.
And if you withhold your money, if you will
not give yourselves, yet if you are but sorry
for your wife at home, if you care for the child
you see in pain, if you stop for the horse who
groans in its galloping, Jesus accepts that love;
He is glad of anything that is a beginning.
Keep the heart soft, keep that place open.
But remember, that for every work of pity
undone, the heart becomes harder; and with
every work of pity done, the heart becomes a
little softer; and if you persevere to do the
thing, it will bring you—you know it will not
save or cleanse you—but somehow it will bring

you, yes, to have pity upon yourselves, to have a soft heart into which the grace of Christ can enter like a healing wine. Christ will take anything—anything rather than nothing; anything rather than it should be said at the last day that we had paid nothing into the treasury, where everything is preserved, and small things become great. At the last day He would fain have something of yours to show, that He may say to the Father, "Behold, they gave Me a cup of cold water. Inasmuch as they did it unto the least of these my brethen, they did it unto Me." And the soul which has had pity upon the weak shall scarcely be lost. When they are done truly in Christ's name, such works of mercy win the reward which is due to Christ—eternal life.

But to return; for our poor souls we need our fulfilment of the mystery of Christ's thirst. We must not be surprised that after our joy, after happy experiences of faith, we come back to the drudgery of common life, come back to the thirst, and come back to its satisfaction. We must have this kind of discipline, this kind of mortification, if we are to go on to that of which I hope just now to speak. We pursue the true track, and we are one with the Saviour only as we accept that discipline. Let us, day by day, seek to renew our knowledge of God's face—seek to renew our brotherly community in the Church—seek to renew our patient bearing of pain—seek first of all and always to renew our peace with God, by pleading freshly, day by day, the availing merits of our Saviour's Passion; and on this foundation let us receive the weight of discipline as the prepared course upon which the building of a Christian life may rest.

THE SIXTH WORD

IT IS FINISHED

"When Jesus therefore had received the vinegar, He said, It is finished."—St. John xix. 30.

It was God's Will that was finished. It was that which He accepted in His Human Nature, as His meat and drink, to do the Father's Will. This Will of the Father was now finished, and Jesus Christ was content. And from this we learn what it is that as penitents we still need. We have spoken as if we went on steadily from point to point. There will be many difficulties, backslidings, failings, the enemy of souls bringing harder and harder trials to bear upon us just in proportion as we are really making spiritual progress. And so time after time we must be content to begin again at the beginning, knowing that we have no hope but hope for pardon in our guilt; that we are sinners condemned, and ask for no privilege, no spiritual accomplishments, but only that God may for Christ's sake once

again forgive us our sins. Yet in spite of all
our badness, as we go on in Him continually
renewed in pardon, there will be a progress,
and there is a point when we shall come to
need just the special lesson of this word. The
mind has escaped from a state of wretchedness
and wilful enmity to God, to pass to a laborious
bearing of pain, to a real fellowship in the
Church, to a holy knowledge of God, to a
willing bearing of all the different burdens
which God uses for the working out of His
plan. After all this a man may come to be
able to grasp one simple thought, to desire
God's will *because it is God's will*. That is by
no means a state which comes without saying,
which comes without a trial. We first of all
desire cleanliness because it is clean, and are
glad that there is God to give us the cleanliness which we choose. And then we advance
so as to desire work of various kinds; work
for the heathen, for the poor. We are on fire
for some special enterprise, some chosen object.
It is not till later for the most part that
men have grace to accept the Will of God
because it is the Will of God, not knowing
what that Will may be. But as the Spirit
of Jesus conquers in them; as out of the root
of a heart bound up into His Heart by the
cord of love there flow out streams of healing
for the mind and conscience; gradually more

and more the man is content to accept
opportunities of service which his own impulse would never have chosen. He desires
no longer what is easiest, he desires no
longer even what is hard. He will not go
where sacrifice might be splendid or where
service seems most needed. He desires only
God's Will—what it is, as it is, not knowing
what it is. That is His meat and drink, to be
doing what God wishes, even if it seems like
rest. That is a great advance. It is much
further advanced than the state of the man
who is ever ready to throw himself into the
breach, who is ever ready for the forlorn hope.
This is the spirit of God's servant, willing to
receive honour or dishonour, able to be full as
well as able to be empty, able to bear praise as
well as able to bear blame; doing all things
through Christ that strengtheneth him; doing
all things in the Spirit of Christ, because they
are the Father's Will. Pray we for that. That
is the security of the penitent life—to be able
to accept the Father's will for what it is. Too
often it is to us dark and hard and severe; we
dread to touch it; it seems to us unknown
and obscure so that we fear to commit ourselves to it. But remember, we know what it
is, we know where it ends. We have the two-
fold revelation of its character. It is our
sanctification and it is His glory. And while

we know it by report, being told that His Will is our sanctification, we know it also by inspection in Jesus Christ. There, in the Man who *did* God's will, we know what God's will is. Is it a thing to shrink from ? Perfect love, perfect sacrifice, perfect brotherhood, perfect generosity, perfect communion with the Father. We know the outlet of that stream. We know how it debouches into the ocean of heavenly love. Therefore we ought not to fear the dark channels of its higher fountains. It is as we cross it like one of those dark rock-hewn passages for water which you may see filled from the highland lakes, where the river runs black between the perpendicular sides of crowding mountains. So the Will appears to us ; dark, unfathomable, forbidding, cold, leading we know not where. But cast the mind ahead ; cast the eye of faith in front ; see where it becomes the river of water of life, broad rivers of water by the golden city of peace, where is the home of God's love, the perfection of sacrifice—the joy of an accomplished service. And take the Will now as you find it though it leads you through dark places, through dull routine, through unwelcome effort, through times of invalidship, through home life when you would gladly be with the heathen, through society when you would gladly be with the poor. Take it as it comes ;

it will lead out into broader passages. It is
ours only to grasp steadily the clue. Seize
hold of the love of God, which is His Will.
Only seize hold of the Will of God in Jesus
Christ, and the path you tread will lead out
into broad ways of abundance, into plenteous
accomplishments of sacrifice, into perfect
burning up of self, into vigorous life within
the Heart of God. That must be the clinching
of your penitence—I choose God's Will *because it is His Will*. There can be therefore
no complaint, no discontent, no weariness. I
have only to hold myself together and He will
take me as I am with that which is good in
me by His gift, and with that which is bad in
me by my own fault; and he will take it all
that He may burn the bad in the fire and put
the good in His garner. All is His, and I
have only this to learn, that the world is His.
The path I tread is now sanctified, not because
it has been changed outwardly, but because I
who tread along it am offered. Now all the
ways of life are the paths which God has
created for me to walk in, and all the tasks of
the week are the good works which He hath
prepared for me to do. If only the life, the
future, be in Jesus Christ offered to God, then
we may go forward in a perfect contentment,
and each thing and each person we meet is
the person God sends us, the thing God
would have us do. His will is enough for us;

3

so that we tread forward in joy knowing clearly only our higher aims; not fretful because there seems no splendour of sacrifice in our lives. And as we thus walk along what seems the prosaic path, if only we walk in the spirit of those who have been offered, we may say at the end—"It is finished. I have finished the work that Thou gavest me to do, for I have finished that which came, and I believe that Thou leddest me to it; Thou didst give it me to do. Only make me Thine own and all the circumstances are Thy task. And if I but tread through them by Thy grace, I may say, Thou hast given me the work; and I have finished the work that Thou didst give me to do."

Set this in line with your penitence. Know this to be the stamp of pardon, the seal of absolution; and be sure that no accomplishment of daily duty, no renewal of your task, can be done without the renewal of the pardon which lays open the gate of revelation to you, brings you into that great household where there is no waste, brings you to the Father to receive your orders, sets you forth bearing His burden, bearing His yoke, that yoke which fits so close in order that by its help you may draw the heavy burden of the cross of His Will unto the accomplishment which He has designed and to which He invites you.

THE SEVENTH WORD

FATHER, INTO THY HANDS I COMMEND MY SPIRIT

"And when Jesus had cried with a loud voice, He said, Father, into Thy Hands I commend My spirit: and having said thus, He gave up the ghost."—St. Luke xxiii. 46.

He said of Himself, "No man taketh My life from Me but I lay it down of Myself." And so now in the energy of His Holy Will, He relinquisheth His soul gladly into the hands of the Father. And think. Those Hands were round Him all His life. There was no void through which His soul must lapse into the Father's Hands. There was no moment as it fled from His body before it reached its home, its support. But it had ever all through life been clasped by that strength. "Underneath are the everlasting arms"; and in truth He had simply to leave those things which seemed to stand between Him and the Father, so that the soul which had always been supported by the Father might be supported by Him alone

—might remain safe in His Hands Who had always held it up. Let us think thus of the Lord committing His soul into the hands of its Creator—the soul which had never slipped from God's holy guardianship. For He teaches by this our last need in the road of penitence. After pardon, patience; after patience, home; after home, communion; after communion, discipline; after discipline, singleness of aim to take up the work because it is God's will. And what remains? But one thing more—to lay it down. That is all. After labour, rest; after pain, refreshment. And we have to learn that God pursues us with His mercy even to our weariness. And when we have accepted His work from Him and borne as best we might, borne it by His grace; then for our last duty He invites us to rest. He makes even the relinquishment of toil a work of submission to Him, so that when we cease from labour we may not cease from obedience, but may rest at His commandment, even as at His commandment we struggle and persevere. See the wondrous mercy of God; that He allows no man to wait for His goodness; that He makes His refreshment a duty; that He makes rest an answer to His commandment. So be sure when you have taken up the work, He will bid you rest. And it may be that not long after you have really accepted it, it will be the time for its relinquishment. And the relinquishment shall be sweet; and the sleep shall be welcome to you; the sleep which God gives to His beloved. And the soul which has borne discipline, which has cast out sin, shall lie at rest, shall fall asleep in Jesus Christ; shall willingly lay itself to sleep, not away from God, to be caught by God, but in God. It shall see the things of sense pass away while the sure hold of God which we have known in this life shall hold us still safe, and we shall rest for evermore in a peace which shall be full of blessing because full of obedience—a peace which is the very accomplishment of His whole aim in us.

In earlier steps Christ wins us blessing by accepting the curse. We have our peace through the chastisement which fell on Him, our healing by His stripes, our consolation in pain through His refusal to come down from the Cross. He saveth others because Himself He will not save. Our home was built by His bereavement, our communion by His desolation, even our heroism by His acceptance of relief. But as we draw near the end, the deeper truth alone abides our statement. It is no longer " Christ instead of us," but " Christ in us." We see that the nearer secret of His Passion is life—life for all; the life of

all in union with His own. And so, no longer
in contrast but in harmony, His love of the
Divine Will, the Father's work, is our acceptance of the purpose, our obedience to the
call; and our rest is no rest except it be the
very rest of Him Who, having done all things,
sat down at the right hand of power.

Thus, from the first step to the last, does
the Divine Love carry the poor sinner from
the confusion of his crime and folly to the
eternal peace of God's children, by the precious
Blood-shedding of Jesus Christ our Lord.

THE END

PRINTED IN GREAT BRITAIN BY RICHARD CLAY & SONS, LIMITED,
BRUNSWICK ST., STAMFORD ST., S.E. 1, AND BUNGAY, SUFFOLK.